A Collection of Classic Chinese Poems and Lyrics

中国经典诗词选英译

[汉英对照]

尹绍东 译著

Compiled & translated by Yin Shaodong

中国人民大学出版社
·北京·

图书在版编目（CIP）数据

中国经典诗词选英译 /尹绍东译著. —北京：中国人民大学出版社，2019.9
ISBN 978-7-300-27432-4

Ⅰ.①中… Ⅱ.①尹… Ⅲ.①古典诗歌–诗集–中国–英文 Ⅳ.①I222

中国版本图书馆 CIP 数据核字（2019）第 198677 号

中国经典诗词选英译

尹绍东　译著

Zhongguo Jingdian Shicixuan Yingyi

出版发行	中国人民大学出版社			
社　　址	北京中关村大街 31 号		邮政编码	100080
电　　话	010-62511242（总编室）		010-62511770（质管部）	
	010-82501766（邮购部）		010-62514148（门市部）	
	010-62515195（发行公司）		010-62515275（盗版举报）	
网　　址	http://www.crup.com.cn			
经　　销	新华书店			
印　　刷	北京昌联印刷有限公司			
规　　格	170 mm×240 mm　16 开本		版　次	2019 年 9 月第 1 版
印　　张	14.75		印　次	2020 年 10 月第 2 次印刷
字　　数	276 000		定　价	58.00 元

版权所有　　侵权必究　　印装差错　　负责调换

序

翻译，是语言转换，但不是语言符号之间的简单替换。相反，它最终是文化转换，是对译出语语料的分析与解构和对译入语内容的重组与构建，是语言与文化的高度融合。

当今，科学技术高度发展，人工智能技术日趋成熟，翻译行业受到严重挑战，尤其是简单的日常交流能借助机器实现，一般的非文学翻译能借助语料库实现高匹配翻译，一般的文学翻译也能基本实现。

然而，机器是翻译不了古典诗歌的，因为古典诗歌语言过于凝练，因为诗歌语汇过于古雅，因为诗歌语言词义古今不同，因为诗歌表达的感情丰富至极，因为诗歌是一个情感世界。我认为，它也是人类最高的生活境界。

有人还在讨论诗歌的可译性，实在无必要。实际上，诗歌翻译始终没有停止过，并且翻译水平越来越高。然而，诗歌翻译的确很难。弗罗斯特曾说："Poetry is what gets lost in translation（诗，翻译所失也）"。他不仅指出诗歌翻译的艰难，还指出误译的不可避免性。的确，我认为，凡是翻译，都有误译，即便理解正确，不恰当的表达也仍然存在。完全对等的翻译是不存在的。

诗歌翻译在文化建设上一直起着十分重要的作用。在对外国诗歌进行汉译中，无论使用古文还是白话文，都在不同时期起到重要作用，或鼓舞斗志，或教人爱国，或展示爱情，或讴歌自然，对中国诗歌艺术是一种丰富。同样，中国诗歌的外译，无论是外国人译的还是中国人译的，都促进了外国对中国诗歌文化、伦理、社会风俗的了解，都促进了世界文化的交流。

中国诗歌英译是传播中国文化的重要途径，是东学西渐和帮助其他国家更多了解中国的重要手段。诗歌是中国历代文学的精华所在，承载了中华文化的基因，反映了中华民族的文化精神和不同历史时期诗人的情怀和信仰。

《诗经》，集黄河流域民歌、贵族祭祀之歌和宗庙祭祀之歌为一体，反映了周朝约五百年间的社会生活面貌。战国后期，《楚辞》出现在长江流域的楚国，标志着诗歌从民间集体创作发展到诗人独立创作的阶段。《诗经》和《楚辞》，是中国诗歌发展的两大源头，共同开创了中国古代诗歌现实主义和浪漫主义和谐发展的传统。

乐府诗在两汉时期逐渐达到鼎盛，魏晋南北朝时期创作不断，形成了唐诗和宋词的雏形。

唐代是中国诗歌史上的黄金时代，流派纷呈，名家辈出，成就卓著。

宋代文学以词为主。宋初，词多写个人离愁。苏轼扩大了词的题材，提高了词的意境，丰富了词的表现手法，开创了豪放词派。辛弃疾使宋词的思想境界和精神面貌达到了前所未有的高度，在词的艺术表现手法上有了新的突破和发展。宋后期，词复归婉约。秦观之词柔婉清丽，情辞兼胜。李清照善于炼字炼意，擅长白描。宋末期，文天祥等人的爱国诗篇，为宋代诗坛添上了最后一抹光彩。

元代以散曲而著名。元曲扩展了诗歌的表现范围，经常与前代诗词互文，形式自由，语言活泼，口语性强，还有地域特征，雅俗共赏，接地气，给诗坛注入了一股清新空气。

明清以小说著称于世。除杨慎、龚自珍和纳兰性德等人外，明、清两朝有影响力的诗人为数不多。龚自珍之诗揭社会之黑暗，抒报国之大志，赢得"三百年来第一流"（柳亚子语）的称誉。

现当代诗人辈出，但把个人之志与家国情怀结合最完美的当属毛泽东。毛泽东诗词是中国革命和建设的史诗，秉承爱国主义传统，具有强烈时代特色，反映中华民族精神，体现共产党人初心，抒发远大革命理想，成为现代中国精神的文化符号，成为全世界作品出版发行数量最大、阅读群体最大的诗人。

在中国三千年的诗歌长河中，经典诗词是中华民族精神追求的深沉积淀，是中华民族生生不息、发展壮大的丰厚滋养。经典诗词伴随一代又一代人成长，滋养了中华民族的民族精神。

经典诗词英译是中华文化对外传播的重要组成部分。对中国诗词进行外译的历史悠久，译者各显神通，把中国诗词文化传播到世界各地，与世界文明互鉴，与世界文化共存。然而，随着时代的变迁和理解的加深，对诗词进行重译，也是有必要的。尹绍东老师的《中国经典诗词选英译》则是这一环节上的一朵小花。

我与云南高校外语界尤其是云南师范大学外国语学院友谊至深，常去云南，或上课，或讲座，或采风，结交了许多有学问、有情有义、多个民族的学者，其中包括尹绍东老师，窃喜遇见一个志同道合的青年学者、一个值得敬仰的翻译人才。

尹绍东老师治学严谨，有思辨精神和创造性。他参加了李昌银教授主持的"十三五"国家重点出版物出版规划项目"云南少数民族经典作品英译文库"翻译工作，承担了苗族长篇叙事诗《金笛》的翻译。他的译诗忠实、达意、通顺，做到了语言交际与文化传递完美的统一，为民族典籍英译积累了成果。

尹绍东老师精选并翻译了一百首中国经典古诗词，集于一书出版。这些诗词都是脍炙人口的经典之作。他力争用英语表达出这些经典诗歌的意象、意境、音美、形美和神韵，精益求精，敢于创新，形成了自己的特色。

他力求知诗真意，传其真意；知诗神韵，传其神韵。另外，他对许多诗词的理解很有新意。例如，"雎鸠""蒹葭"到底为何物？他遍查资料，寻访专家，认真求证，呈现出自己独特的译文。他没有把"床前明月光"中的"床"译成"bed"，而是译为"around the well"，他是古今中外第一个如此处理的，是一创举。我认为，他对中国古诗词有着自己独到的理解，令人耳目一新。他的翻译是研究型翻译，并且很有说服力。

尹绍东老师对诗词的理解、考证、翻译为我们提供了正确理解这些诗词的另一种选项。我认为，他提供的选项是有道理的。

概括而言，本书有以下特点：

一、符合国际交流的需求。在全球化背景下，向世界讲好中国故事，正确讲述中国故事，推动中国文化走出去，让世界了解中国，这已成为当代中国的国家战略。中国文学，尤其是古典文学的英译，正是这一战略的重要组成部分。古典诗词的英译，可以帮助外国读者进一步了解悠久的中国文学传统和辉煌的文学成就，从而对中国文化有更全面、更深刻的认识，继而实现文明互鉴和民心相通。

二、所选作品代表性强。本书选编了自先秦以降两千多年来的经典诗词，从《诗经》《楚辞》到毛泽东诗词，各个时代、各种风格的代表作均有入选。重点考虑历代大师的经典作品，如李白、杜甫、苏轼、辛弃疾、李清照、毛泽东等，兼顾其他诗人的佳作名篇。其中，有三件作品的入选令人耳目一新。

第一、刘禹锡的《陋室铭》。按照传统的文类划分，铭文自成一体，既不是诗，也不是文。但有一点值得注意，铭文属于韵文，并不是严格意义上的散体。从这个意义上讲，《陋室铭》的收录具有创新价值，同时又有依据。

第二、明代文学家杨慎的《临江仙·滚滚长江东逝水》。这是杨慎所作《廿一史弹词》第三段《说秦汉》的开场词，后清初毛宗岗父子评刻《三国演义》时将其移至《三国演义》卷首，20世纪90年代电视剧《三国演义》将其作为主题曲广泛传播，知名度非常高。译者将其选入，可谓独具慧眼。

第三、罗庸的《西南联大校歌》。歌词采用"满江红"词牌格式写成，悲壮典雅，感人至深。该词的入选具有特殊意义，表达了译者对联大光辉历史的敬意和作为联大遗脉的云南师大一分子的自豪。以上三首作品的入选使本书超越了同类的其他选本，成为独树一帜的汉诗英译选集。

三、译文质量高。选集收录的一百首中国经典诗词，均属韵体，而译文也采用韵体，不仅诗行讲究节奏，行末也尽量押韵，音乐性强，朗朗上口。总体上看，译文从信、达、雅三个方面再现了原文的主题内容、形式特征和语言风格，是汉诗英译之以诗译诗的又一重要成果。当然，译文不可能都是十全十美的，因为每个读者都有自己的期待，但只要理解正确，即便表达上有些不足之处，也应包容。

　　这本诗集英译的出现是中国古诗词英译领域一件值得关注的事情，因为这本书的出版将大大丰富中西方读者对中国经典诗词的理解，给诗歌翻译活动带来一定启示。

　　译本出版之际，他所在学院领导和他本人邀我通读书稿，嘱我作序。仓促之间，寥寥数语，难言其妙。请读者读后自评。

　　是为序。

李正栓 博士、教授

河北师范大学外国语学院

中国英汉语比较研究会典籍英译专业委员会常务副会长兼秘书长

2019 年 6 月 6 日

PREFACE

Translation is a transformation of one language into another, but not the simple substitution of language symbols. Instead, it is, in the end, cultural transformation. Translation is achieved through an analysis and deconstruction of the source language materials and the reorganization and construction of the content in the target language. In this way, an advanced integration of language and culture is produced.

In such an age when science and technology are highly developed, and artificial intelligence is increasingly perfected, the translation industry is being greatly challenged. Simple daily communications between people from different languages can be done through machine translation. Ordinary non-literary translation can be fulfilled with relative accuracy with the help of corpus, and general literary translation can be almost realized.

However, machines cannot translate classical poetry, since the language used in classical poetry is more condensed, and the vocabulary is more classical and elegant, as well as the fact that the meanings of words have been undergoing changes over time. Furthermore, profound emotions abound in poetry, so poetry is an emotional world, and in my opinion, it is also the highest realm of human life.

It is still debated whether poetry is translatable or untranslatable, and I believe the debate is really unnecessary. Poetry should be translated whether it is translatable or untranslatable. In fact, the translation of poetry has never stopped, and the quality of translation has become higher and higher. However, poetry translation is indeed difficult. Robert Frost once said that "poetry is what gets lost in translation." He has not only pointed out the difficulty of poetry translation, but also the fact that mistranslation is unavoidable. In fact, I believe, there are always mistranslations in translation of any kind. Even if a poem has been correctly understood, improper expressions still exist in translation. Absolute equivalence in translation is a castle in the air.

Poetry translation has been playing an important role in cultural construction. Chinese translation of foreign poetry, either into classical Chinese or modern Mandarin, has greatly and deeply influenced Chinese people at different times. The foreign poems translated are either encouraging or patriotic. They show us what love is about or sing highly of nature. This has enriched Chinese poetry. Meanwhile, foreign translations of Chinese poetry, whether translated by foreign scholars or Chinese translators, have all promoted foreigners' understanding of Chinese poetry culture, ethics, and social customs, and stimulated exchange between world cultures.

Translating Chinese poetry into English is an important way to spread Chinese culture, and it is also a vital means to introduce Chinese culture to the West and help other countries know more about China. Poetry is the essence of Chinese literature in history and it has carried the DNA of the Chinese culture and reflected the cultural spirit of the Chinese people, as well as the poets' sentiments and beliefs throughout Chinese history.

The Book of Songs includes folk songs of the Yellow River Basin, ceremonial or festive odes of the nobles and ritual hymns of sacrifice to praise ancestors. It reflects the social life of the Western and Eastern Zhou Dynasties within a period of about five hundred years. In the late years of the Warring Period, *The Verse of the Chu*, which originated in the Kingdom of Chu in the Yangtze River Basin, indicated that poetry writing had shifted from a collective product to an individual one. *The Book of Songs* and *The Verse of the Chu* are the two origins of Chinese poetry, and they together have established the tradition of the harmonious coexistence of realism and romanticism in classical Chinese poetry.

During the Western and Eastern Han Dynasties, Music-Bureau poetry[①] achieved great success and blossomed. In the Wei and Jin Periods and the Southern and Northern Dynasties, Music-Bureau poetry continued to develop, thus becoming the embryo of

---

① During the Qin Dynasty (221BC–206 BC) in Chinese history, the **Imperial Music Bureau** was established. It was an organization that united musical practices throughout China and organized the folk songs into court and military music. Its purpose was to collect regional popular music and poetry, oversee ceremonies at court, hire musicians, and standardize pitch (A version of this office continued to operate until 1911.) Later during the Han Dynasty, in Emperor Wu's time, the **Music Bureau** was greatly expanded. Many ancient traditions lost during the Qin Dynasty were recovered, and a Confucian musical ideology was disseminated. The **Music Bureau** was officially disbanded by Emperor Ai of Han in the year 7 BC, partly as an economy measure. By that time, it had nearly 830 musicians and dancers. The **Music Bureau** was not revived for a long period. During the Tang Dynasty, the **Music Bureau** was also responsible for composing music for the Grand Carnival in the capital city Chang'an. Music in Tang-dynasty China underwent a radical change in the sixth and seventh centuries as a result of the mass migration of peoples from Central Asia, many of whom came to the interior of China as musicians and dancers at the imperial court.

PREFACE

the Tang poetry and the Song lyrics.

The Tang Dynasty was the golden age in the history of Chinese poetry and witnessed the prosperity of different schools and brilliant poets, who were at the peak of achievement in Chinese poetry writing.

Lyrics were the typical literature of the Song Dynasty. In the early Song Dynasty, lyrics were mainly about personal sadness or melancholy over parting. Su Shi broadened the scope of lyrics, elevated their artistic conception, enriched their expression and created the "School of Heroic Abandon." With Xin Qiji's appearance, lyrics reached their apex in the realm of thought and spiritual outlook. This was unprecedented in the history of poetry. In the artistic expressions of lyrics, there were breakthroughs in poetry development. In the late Song Dynasty, lyrics became delicate and restrained again. Qin Guan's lyrics were soft, delicate and beautiful, while Li Qingzhao was a genius in word choice and refinement and was quite good at poetical sketches. At the end of the Song Dynasty, Wen Tianxiang's and some other poets' patriotic poems were the final splendor of poetry in the Song Dynasty.

The Yuan Dynasty was known for its dramatic songs. Yuan songs broadened the scope of poetry expression and very often, there was intertextuality between dramatic songs and poems in previous dynasties. Dramatic songs are free in form and lively in language. The use of everyday colloquial speech was common in dramatic songs and regional characteristics could be found in their language, thus being loved by both the literati and the common people. In their closeness to daily life, dramatic songs have brought a breath of fresh air to poetry writing.

The Ming and the Qing Dynasties were famous for novels. Except for Yang Shen, Gong Zizhen and Nalan Xingde, there were few influential poets during the two dynasties. Gong Zizhen's poems exposed the darkness of society and expressed his great ambition to serve the country, thus earning him the reputation of being "a first-class poet in three hundred years" (by Liu Yazi).

In modern and contemporary China, poets have come out in large numbers, but Mao Zedong was the only one who perfectly merged his personal aspirations with his love for the nation and country. Mao Zedong's poems are epics of Chinese revolution and construction, and have inherited traditional patriotism. They have striking characteristics of the times and reflect the spirit of the Chinese people and the original aspiration of the Communist Party of China. Mao Zedong's poems express his great revolutionary ideals and have become cultural symbols of the spirit of modern China.

He was the poet whose poems enjoyed the most widespread publication with readers around the world.

For 3,000 years, in the long river of Chinese poetry, classic poems have been an impressive accumulation of Chinese spiritual aspiration and the rich soil for the growth and development of the Chinese people. Classic poems have been with Chinese people for generations and have nourished their national spirit.

The English translation of classic poems is an important part of spreading Chinese culture to foreign countries. There has been a long history of translating Chinese poetry into foreign languages. The translators have tried what they could to spread Chinese poetic culture to the world, and share or draw on all the achievements of world civilizations. It is their wish to make Chinese poetic culture part of world cultures. However, with the changing times and research done on poems, it is really necessary to retranslate them. Mr. Yin Shaodong's *A Collection of Classic Chinese Poems and Lyrics* is a little flower among those translation works.

I have formed close friendships with the foreign language circle in colleges and universities in Yunnan, particularly the School of Foreign Languages and Literature of Yunnan Normal University. I have been to Yunnan very often for classes, or lectures, or field studies, and have made friends with many learned and sincere scholars of different nationalities, one of whom is Mr. Yin Shaodong. I am very happy to meet a young scholar, an admirable talent in translation, who has a common interest with me.

Mr. Yin Shaodong is a speculative and creative scholar with a rigorous and inquiring mind. He has taken part in the project led by Professor Li Changyin, "Classics of Yunnan Ethnic Groups in English Translation." This project is part of "The Thirteenth Five-Year Plan for Key National Publication Program." He has translated *Gold Flute*, an epic of the Hmong people, and his translation is faithful, expressive and smooth. In his translation, he has achieved the perfect integration of language communication and cultural transmission, and has thus made a contribution to the English translation of ethnic classics.

Mr. Yin Shaodong has selected and translated one hundred classic Chinese poems, which will be published. These poems are classics which have been popular and widely praised one generation after another among Chinese people. He tried to convey in English the images, artistic conception, the beauty of sound and form and the romantic charm of these classic Chinese poems. When translating the poems, he constantly strived for perfection and creativity in the formation of unique characteristics in the

English translation of Chinese poems.

He has made every effort to know a poem's true meaning, convey its true meaning in English, know a poem's romantic charm and convey its romantic charm in English. Moreover, he has a new and fresh understanding of many poems. For instance, what really are "*jujiu*" and "*jianjia*"? He searched for materials, consulted experts, conducted serious research and finally presented his own unique translation to us. He did not translate "*chuang*" in Li Bai's "*chuang qian ming yue guang*" as "bed," instead, he used the phrase "around the well" to convey the meaning of "*chuang*." He is the first translator in the world to deal with the word in such a way. It is my idea that he has his own unique understanding of classical Chinese poetry. His translation is based on research and it is very persuasive and convincing.

Mr. Yin Shaodong's understanding, textual research and translation have provided us with another way to correctly understand these poems. I believe that the different ways he offered are very convincing.

Broadly speaking, his book has the following features:

1. **It meets the requirements for international communication.** In the context of globalization, it is China's national strategy to relate, in good ways, Chinese stories to the world. These Chinese stories should also be correctly told to introduce Chinese culture to foreign countries and help the world know more about China. The English translation of Chinese literature, particularly classical literature, is one of the most important parts of the strategy. English translation of classical Chinese poetry can help international readers further understand the long Chinese literary tradition and China's glorious literary achievement. In this way, they can have a more thorough and deeper understanding of Chinese culture. This will enable different civilizations to know and emulate each other and people from different countries will be closer to each other.

2. **The poems selected are representative.** The collection includes classic poems from the Pre-Qin Period to the modern times, with a time span of over 2,000 years. The works selected include poems from *The Book of Songs*, and *The Verse of the Chu* to Mao Zedong, covering each period of Chinese history and different styles. The majority of classic poems selected are from master poets like Li Bai, Du Fu, Su Shi, Xin Qiji, Li Qingzhao, Mao Zedong, as well as classic poems of other poets. Among the works selected, three poems, like a breath of fresh air, are well worth mentioning.

Firstly, Liu Yuxi's *An Epigraph on the Simple House*, according to traditional literary division, is neither a poem nor an article. It is an epigraph, so different from other literary styles. However, it should be pointed out that an epigraph makes use of rhymed verse, so it is not, in a strict sense, prose. From this point of view, the appearance of *An Epigraph on the Simple House* in a poetry collection, which is well-founded, will be a fresh reading experience for readers.

Secondly, *Tune to "Riverside Daffodils"· Rolling, Rolling, the Yangtze River Flows Eastward*, a lyric poem from Yang Shen, a Ming Dynasty writer, is in fact, the opening words of *On the Qin and the Han Dynasties*. This third part of the fiddle ballads *Twenty-one Dynasties* is sung in Chinese southern dialects. Later, in the early Qing Dynasty, when Mao Zonggang and his father commented on the *Romance of the Three Kingdoms*, written by Luo Guanzhong, and published their version, they borrowed the lyric poem and put it at the beginning of the *Romance of the Three Kingdoms*. In the 1990s, it was used as the theme song of the TV series the *Romance of the Three Kingdoms*, so it has become widely known all over China. The translator can see what others cannot for the very fact that his selection is really unique.

Thirdly, the selection of the *Anthem of National Southwestern Associated University*, written by Luo Yong, is another example that makes the present collection so special. The lyric, written to the tune "*Red Water Fern*," is grave, elegant, and touching. The selection of this lyric poem has special significance, indicating the translator's respect for the glorious history of the National Southwestern Associated University and his pride in being a part of Yunnan Normal University. This collection excels similar ones because of the inclusion of these three poems. Mr. Yin Shaodong has blazed a trail in selecting classic Chinese poems for English translation.

3. **The translation of the collection is of high quality.** The one hundred classic Chinese poems in the collection are almost all rhymed, and their English translations are also almost rhymed. Each line of the English version is rhythmic, and the translator has tried hard to get the ending word in each line to rhyme, which makes his version beautifully musical with a captivating tune. Overall, his translation has reproduced each original poem's thematic content, form, characteristics and language style in terms of faithfulness, expressiveness, and elegance. Therefore, it can be seen as an important product of the English translation of Chinese poetry. Undoubtedly, the translation can never be as perfect as the translator wishes, since every reader has his/her own expectations. However, as long as the translator is correct in his understanding of the poems, it is understandable that there might be some flaws in his translation, which, I think, should be tolerated.

PREFACE

    The present collection of the English translation of Chinese poetry is well worth paying attention to in the circle of the English translation of classical Chinese poetry whether in the West or in China, the publication of the book will greatly enrich readers' understanding of classic Chinese poems. The book will also provide some enlightenment to the English translation of Chinese poetry.

    On the verge of its publication, it was expected of me by the translator's director in the School of Foreign Languages and Literature of Yunnan Normal University and the translator himself to read through the draft and write a foreword for the collection. Within a limited time, it is hard for this short piece to tell in detail the charm of Mr. Yin Shaodong's translation. The readers are expected to find them all by themselves.

    This short piece of work serves as the foreword.

Li Zhengshuan Ph.D & Professor
School of Foreign Studies of Hebei Normal University
Standing Vice Chairman and Secretary General of
Classics Translation Committee of CACSEC
6 June 2019

CONTENTS

佚名 Anonymous
1. 国风·周南·关雎 ·· 2
Folk Songs·A Folk Song from the Southern Region under the Rule of the Duke of Zhou·The Courting White-breasted Waterhen

佚名 Anonymous
2. 国风·秦风·蒹葭 ·· 4
Folk Songs·A Folk Song from the Region under the Rule of the Duke of Qin·Earless Reeds and Shoots

屈原 Qu Yuan
3. 九歌·国殇 ·· 6
Nine Songs·An Elegy on Deaths of Servicemen Who Sacrificed Their Lives for the Country

项羽 Xiang Yu
4. 垓下歌 ··· 8
Song of Gaixia

虞姬 Yu Ji
5. 和垓下歌 ··· 10
Reply to King Xiang's Song

刘邦 Liu Bang
6. 大风歌 ··· 12
Song of a Gale

1

毛苹 Mao Ping
7. 上邪 ··· 14
   O Heaven

曹操 Cao Cao
8. 龟虽寿 ·· 16
   Though the Tortoise Enjoys Longevity

曹植 Cao Zhi
9. 七步诗 ·· 18
   A Poem Written in Seven Steps

陶渊明 Tao Yuanming
10. 归园田居（其一）·· 20
    Returning to Yuantianju Dwelling (1st Poem)
11. 饮酒 ·· 22
    Drinking

北朝民歌 A Folk Song of the Northern Dynasties
12. 敕勒歌 ··· 24
    Song of Chi'le Nationality

王勃 Wang Bo
13. 送杜少府之任蜀州 ·· 26
    To See Police Commissioner Du Off for Shuzhou City

陈子昂 Chen Zi'ang
14. 登幽州台歌 ·· 28
    Song of Ascending the You Prefecture Tower

张若虚 Zhang Ruoxu
15. 春江花月夜 ·· 30
    A Flower-and-Moon Night on the Spring River

王翰 Wang Han
16. 凉州词 ··· 34
    Liangzhou Lyrics

CONTENTS

张九龄 Zhang Jiuling
17. 望月怀远 ·· 36
    Looking at the Moon and Cherishing the Faraway Place

孟浩然 Meng Haoran
18. 宿建德江 ·· 38
    Staying Overnight on the Jiande River
19. 春晓 ·· 40
    Spring Dawn

王之涣 Wang Zhihuan
20. 登鹳雀楼 ·· 42
    Ascending the Stork Tower

贺知章 He Zhizhang
21. 回乡偶书（其一）··· 44
    A Chance Writing When Returning to My Hometown (1st Poem)
22. 回乡偶书（其二）··· 46
    A Chance Writing When Returning to My Hometown (2nd Poem)

崔颢 Cui Hao
23. 黄鹤楼 ·· 48
    The Yellow Crane Tower

王昌龄 Wang Changling
24. 出塞 ·· 50
    Out of the Frontier Fortress

王维 Wang Wei
25. 山居秋暝 ·· 52
    An Autumn Evening in the Mountain Village
26. 鹿柴 ·· 54
    Stick Fence for Deer
27. 相思 ·· 56
    Lovesickness
28. 送元二使安西 ·· 58
    To See Yuan'er Off as an Envoy to An'xi

3

李白 Li Bai

29. 月下独酌（其一）·· 60
    Drinking Alone under the Moon (1st Poem)
30. 月下独酌（其二）·· 62
    Drinking Alone under the Moon (2nd Poem)
31. 行路难·· 64
    Hard Is the Journey
32. 登金陵凤凰台·· 66
    Ascending the Phoenix Terrace of Nanjing
33. 早发白帝城·· 68
    Leaving Baidi City in Early Morning
34. 静夜思·· 70
    Thoughts on a Still Night
35. 赠汪伦·· 72
    To Wang Lun for Seeing Me Off

常建 Chang Jian

36. 题破山寺后禅院·· 74
    About the Buddhist Retreat behind the Poshan Temple

杜甫 Du Fu

37. 春望·· 76
    A Glimpse in Spring
38. 登高·· 78
    Ascending High
39. 春夜喜雨·· 80
    A Good Rain in the Spring Night
40. 蜀相·· 82
    The Chancellor of the Kingdom of Shu

岑参 Cen Shen

41. 白雪歌送武判官归京·· 84
    Song of Snow on Seeing the Aide Mr. Wu Off for the Capital

张志和 Zhang Zhihe

42. 渔歌子·· 86
    Song of the Fisherman

CONTENTS

张继 Zhang Ji
43. 枫桥夜泊 ··· 88
    Anchoring at Night by Maple Bridge

刘长卿 Liu Changqing
44. 逢雪宿芙蓉山主人 ·· 90
    The Host in Whose House I Lodge on a Snowy Day on the Confederate Rose Mountain

孟郊 Meng Jiao
45. 游子吟 ·· 92
    Song of the Traveling Son
46. 慈母吟 ·· 94
    Song of My Loving Mother

柳宗元 Liu Zongyuan
47. 江雪 ·· 96
    River Snow

张籍 Zhang Ji
48. 节妇吟·寄东平李司空师道 ·· 98
    Ode to a Chaste Wife·To Minister Li Shidao of Dongping

元稹 Yuan Zhen
49. 离思 ·· 100
    Thoughts after Departing

刘禹锡 Liu Yuxi
50. 陋室铭 ··· 102
    An Epigraph on the Simple House

白居易 Bai Juyi
51. 琵琶行 ··· 104
    Song of Pipa

崔护 Cui Hu
52. 题都城南庄 ··· 110
    A Poem on a Southern Village in the Capital City

杜牧 Du Mu

53. 江南春 ··· 112
   Spring in Regions South of the Yangtze River

54. 清明 ·· 114
   Tomb Sweeping Day

李商隐 Li Shangyin

55. 锦瑟 ·· 116
   The Painted Se

56. 夜雨寄北 ··· 118
   A Poem Written in the Night Rain to My Wife in the North

佚名 Anonymous

57. 铜官窑瓷器题诗 ··· 120
   A Poem Inscribed on Porcelain from Tongguan Kiln

李煜 Li Yu

58. 虞美人·春花秋月何时了? ·· 122
   Tune to "Beauty Yu"· When Will Spring Flowers and Autumn Moon End This Year?

59. 相见欢·无言独上西楼 ·· 124
   Tune to "A Happy Meeting"·Silent and Alone, Up the West Tower I Climb

范仲淹 Fan Zhongyan

60. 苏幕遮·怀旧 ·· 126
   Tune to "The Head Scarf"·Nostalgia

柳永 Liu Yong

61. 雨霖铃·寒蝉凄切 ··· 128
   Tune to "Bells Ringing in the Rain"·Cicadas Are Mournfully Chirping

晏殊 Yan Shu

62. 浣溪沙·一曲新词酒一杯 ·· 130
   Tune to "The Yarn-washing Stream"·I Drink a Cup When Finishing a New Lyric

欧阳修 Ouyang Xiu

63. 蝶恋花·庭院深深深几许 ·· 132
   Tune to "Butterflies' Love of Flowers"· The Courtyard Is Deep, Yet, How Deep Is It?

CONTENTS

王安石 Wang Anshi
64. 梅花 ·· 134
    Plum Blossom

苏轼 Su Shi
65. 水调歌头·明月几时有 ··· 136
    Tune to "Overture to Song of Water"·When Did the Bright Moon First Appear?
66. 念奴娇·赤壁怀古 ··· 138
    Tune to "The Beautiful Niannu"·Meditation on the Distant Past on the Red Cliffs
67. 江城子·乙卯正月二十日夜记梦 ·· 140
    Tune to "Song of Nanjing"·To Record My Dream on the Night of the 20th of the First Month of the Lunar Year, 1075
68. 临江仙·夜归临皋 ··· 142
    Tune to "Riverside Daffodils"·Returning to Lingao at Night
69. 卜算子·黄州定慧院寓居作 ·· 144
    Tune to "Song of the Fortune-Teller"·A Poem Written at Dinghui Temple Where I Lodge

李之仪 Li Zhiyi
70. 卜算子·我住长江头 ··· 146
    Tune to "Song of the Fortune-Teller"·I Live Upstream of the Yangtze River

岳飞 Yue Fei
71. 满江红·写怀 ··· 148
    Tune to "Red Water Fern"·To Express Emotions

李清照 Li Qingzhao
72. 声声慢·寻寻觅觅 ··· 150
    Tune to "A Note-by-note Slow Song"·Seek Seek, Prowl Prowl
73. 如梦令·常记溪亭日暮 ··· 152
    Tune to "A Dreamlike Short Lyric"·I Often Recall the Evening in a Waterside Pavilion
74. 如梦令·昨夜雨疏风骤 ··· 154
    Tune to "A Dreamlike Short Lyric"·Last Night, the Rain Was Light, the Wind Sudden

7

辛弃疾 Xin Qiji

75. 永遇乐·京口北固亭怀古 ················· 156
    Tune to "Receiving Happy News Forever"·Meditation on the Distant Past at Beigu Pavilion in Jingkou

76. 青玉案·元夕 ····························· 158
    Tune to "Green Jade Tray"·The Lantern Festival

77. 菩萨蛮·书江西造口壁 ···················· 160
    Tune to "The Southern Buddha"·An Inscription on a Wall in Zaokou of Jiangxi

78. 丑奴儿·书博山道中壁 ···················· 162
    Tune to "The Ugly Kid"·A Lyric Written on the Rock Face of Boshan Hill

陆游 Lu You

79. 卜算子·咏梅 ····························· 164
    Tune to "Song of the Fortune-Teller"·On Chinese Plum

80. 钗头凤·红酥手 ··························· 166
    Tune to "A Phoenix Hairpin"·Rosy, Soft Hands

唐婉 Tang Wan

81. 钗头凤·世情薄 ··························· 168
    Tune to "A Phoenix Hairpin"·The World Is Cold

赵师秀 Zhao Shixiu

82. 约客 ····································· 170
    Waiting for a Guest

文天祥 Wen Tianxiang

83. 过零丁洋 ································ 172
    To Pass the Lonely Sea

蒋捷 Jiang Jie

84. 虞美人·听雨 ····························· 174
    Tune to "Beauty Yu"·Listening to the Rain

关汉卿 Guan Hanqing

85. 四块玉·别情 ····························· 176
    Tune to "Four Jades"·The Pain of Parting

CONTENTS

白朴 Bai Pu
86. 天净沙·秋 ·············· 178
Tune to "A Sandless Sky"·Autumn

马致远 Ma Zhiyuan
87. 天净沙·秋思 ·············· 180
Tune to "A Sandless Sky"· Autumn Thought

徐再思 Xu Zaisi
88. 折桂令·春情 ·············· 182
Tune to "A Lyric of Picking Sweet Osmanthus Twigs"·Longing for Love

张可久 Zhang Kejiu
89. 殿前欢·离思 ·············· 184
Tune to "Happiness at the Royal Court"·Thought on Parting

唐珙 Tang Gong
90. 题龙阳县青草湖 ·············· 186
On Green Grass Lake in Longyang County

杨慎 Yang Shen
91. 临江仙·滚滚长江东逝水 ·············· 188
Tune to "Riverside Daffodils"·Rolling, Rolling, the Yangtze River Flows Eastward

纳兰性德 Nalan Xingde
92. 蝶恋花·出塞 ·············· 190
Tune to "Butterflies' Love of Flowers"·Out of the Fortress
93. 浣溪沙·谁念西风独自凉 ·············· 192
Tune to "The Yarn-washing Stream"·In the Chilly West Wind, Who Would Care about the Solitary Me?

龚自珍 Gong Zizhen
94. 己亥杂诗（其五）·············· 194
Miscellaneous Poems Written in the Year 1839 (5th Poem)
95. 己亥杂诗（其九十六）·············· 196
Miscellaneous Poems Written in the Year 1839 (96th Poem)
96. 己亥杂诗（其一百二十五）·············· 198
Miscellaneous Poems Written in the Year 1839 (125th Poem)

9

罗庸 Luo Yong

97. 西南联大校歌·· 200
    Anthem of National Southwestern Associated University

毛泽东 Mao Zedong

98. 沁园春·雪·· 202
    Tune to "Spring in Qinyuan Garden"·Snow
99. 沁园春·长沙·· 204
    Tune to "Spring in Qinyuan Garden"·Changsha
100. 卜算子：咏梅··· 206
    Tune to "Song of the Fortune-Teller"·Ode to Plum Blossoms

参考书目·· 208
后记·· 209

中国经典诗词选英译

作者简介

《诗经》是中国最早的诗歌总集，据传为尹吉甫采集、孔子编订，反映了西周初年至春秋中叶（公元前11世纪—公元前6世纪）的社会生活，绝大部分诗文作者不可考。《诗经》被认为是中国现实主义诗歌的源头，共311篇，其中《风》160篇，《雅》105篇，《颂》40篇，其余6篇仅剩标题，无内容，称为笙诗。

《风》多为民间歌谣，主题涉及爱情、婚姻、农事、政治、战争等；《雅》为上层社会典礼、宴会演唱歌曲；《颂》为祭祀、祈祷、祝颂祖先神灵之诗。

《国风·周南·关雎》是中国文学开篇之作，一般认为是男女情歌。此诗以雎鸠之鸣"起兴"，即"先言他物以引起所咏之辞"（朱熹），以采荇菜的动作变化来体现男子对女子的热烈追求。

"雎鸠"到底为何种鸟？历来众说纷纭；有考证认为，"雎鸠"今为"白腹秧鸡"，本诗选译文采此说！

《国风·秦风·蒹葭》勾勒出一幅"可望不可即"的人生画面和艺术意境。此诗寓意深刻，语言简练，节奏明快，双声叠韵，婉转动人。

有观点认为，此诗意在讥刺秦襄公未能以周礼治理国家，或惋惜招引隐士而不得。现代学者多认为《蒹葭》为爱情诗。

蒹：没长穗芦苇；长穗芦苇为萑（huán）；葭：初生芦苇。

一、国风·周南·关雎

先秦：佚名

关关雎鸠，
在河之洲。
窈窕淑女，
君子好逑。

参差荇菜，
左右流之。
窈窕淑女，
寤寐求之。

求之不得，
寤寐思服。
悠哉悠哉，
辗转反侧。

参差荇菜，
左右采之。
窈窕淑女，
琴瑟友之。

参差荇菜，
左右芼之。
窈窕淑女，
钟鼓乐之。

1. Folk Songs·A Folk Song from the Southern Region under the Rule of the Duke of Zhou·The Courting White-breasted Waterhen

The Pre-Qin Period: Anonymous

"Kwak-kwak" courts the white-breasted waterhen
On the islet of the river;
A gentle and graceful maiden
Is a gentleman's good partner.

Water poppies of length uneven,
From left to right, I try to fish for;
A gentle and graceful maiden,
Awake or asleep, I really adore.

I cannot win the heart of my goddess;
Day and night, she is on my mind.
O, I am restless, I am restless;
I toss and turn in bed for love blind.

Water poppies of length uneven,
From left to right, I try to pluck;
A gentle and graceful maiden,
I play the qin① or the se② to befriend to try my luck.

Water poppies of length uneven,
From left to right, I try to pull out;
A gentle and graceful maiden,
I play bells or drums to tease her out.

---

① **qin:** ch'in, also called guqin (Chinese "ancient zither") or qixianqin (Chinese "seven-stringed zither"). The qin is usually lacquered and is inlaid with 13 dots of ivory, jade, or mother-of-pearl that indicate pitch positions, primarily on the upper melodic string. The silk strings, which are of graduated thickness, are tuned pentatonically, and the thickest string is farthest from the player's body.

② **se:** an ancient Chinese plucked zither. It has 25–50 strings of twisted silk with moveable bridges and a range of up to five octaves. It was an instrument for the elite used in rituals and sacrificial offerings.

二、国风·秦风·蒹葭

先秦：佚名

蒹葭苍苍，
白露为霜。
所谓伊人，
在水一方。

溯洄从之，
道阻且长。
溯游从之，
宛在水中央。

蒹葭萋萋，
白露未晞。
所谓伊人，
在水之湄。

溯洄从之，
道阻且跻。
溯游从之，
宛在水中坻。

蒹葭采采，
白露未已。
所谓伊人，
在水之涘。

溯洄从之，
道阻且右。
溯游从之，
宛在水中沚。

2. Folk Songs·A Folk Song from the Region under the Rule of the Duke of Qin·Earless Reeds and Shoots

Pre-Qin Period: Anonymous

Earless reeds and shoots are thriving;
White dew has become frost.
The dear one I have been missing
Is at the riverbank opposite.

I walk upstream to look for her;
The road is difficult and long to conquer.
I walk downstream to look for her,
But she seems to be in the midst of the river.

Earless reeds and shoots are lushly growing;
The white dew has not dried yet.
The dear one I have been missing
Is at the edge of the riverbank opposite.

I walk upstream to look for her;
The road is difficult, climbing higher and higher.
I walk downstream to look for her,
But she seems to be on the islet in the river.

Earless reeds and shoots are flourishing;
The white dew has not completely dried.
The dear one I have been missing
Is at the opposite waterside.

I walk upstream to look for her;
The road is zigzagging, full of danger.
I walk downstream to look for her,
But she seems to be on the ait in the river.

作者简介

屈原（公元前340年—公元前278年），名平，字原；楚国诗人、政治家。生于楚国丹阳（今湖北秭归）；芈（mǐ）姓，楚武王熊通之子屈瑕后代。

屈原是中国浪漫主义诗歌奠基人，后人称之为"诗魂"。他创作的《楚辞》是中国浪漫主义文学源头，与《诗经》并称"风骚"。

《九歌·国殇》取民间"九歌"祭奠之意，哀悼死难的楚国将士。古人将未满二十岁而夭折的人称为殇，也指未经丧礼的无主之鬼。

按古代葬礼，在战场上"无勇而死"者，不能敛以棺柩，葬入墓域。在秦楚战争中，因战败，死难沙场的楚国将士暴尸荒野；无人替这些死国者操办丧礼、祭祀。放逐中的屈原创作了这不朽名篇，祭奠死难将士。

《九歌·国殇》"通篇直赋其事"（戴震《屈原赋注》）。诗篇情感炽烈、节奏急促、描写直白、凛然悲壮；其阳刚之美，在《楚辞》中独树一帜。

三、九歌·国殇

战国：屈原

操吴戈兮披犀甲，
车错毂兮短兵接。
旌蔽日兮敌若云，
矢交坠兮士争先。
凌余阵兮躐余行，
左骖殪兮右刃伤。
霾两轮兮絷四马，
援玉枹兮击鸣鼓。
天时怼兮威灵怒，
严杀尽兮弃原野。
出不入兮往不反，
平原忽兮路超远。
带长剑兮挟秦弓，
首身离兮心不惩。
诚既勇兮又以武，
终刚强兮不可凌。
身既死兮神以灵，
魂魄毅兮为鬼雄。

3. Nine Songs · An Elegy on Deaths of Servicemen Who Sacrificed Their Lives for the Country

The Warring States Period: Qu Yuan

Holding the Wu Kingdom's dagger-axes, O our soldiers were in rhino hide armor;
Chariots charging and clashing, O they grappled with the enemy at close quarters.
War flags obstructing the sun, O the enemy surged forward like storm;
Arrows falling in showers, O our soldiers fought fearlessly in crowds.
The commanding general attacked, O on the enemy he treaded;
The horse on his left was killed, O the one on the right wounded.
Two wheels of his chariot sank into the ground, O his four horses stuck together;
Holding jade-inlaid sticks, O the commanding general struck the war drum harder.
Heaven was irritated; O august gods were enraged at the combat's bloodiness;
All the soldiers cruelly killed, O their bodies were discarded in the wilderness.
When leaving for war, O they had not the least idea of coming home;
The plain was boundless, O the expedition was endless.
They girded on long swords; O they carried the Qin Kingdom's quality bows;
They were decapitated, O but their hearts would never regret or roam.
They were courageous, O they were mighty;
They were always unyielding; O they could never be humiliated.
They are dead, O but their spirits live on eternally.
Their souls are indomitable, O they are heroes among the departed.

四、垓下歌

秦朝：项羽

力拔山兮气盖世，
时不利兮骓不逝。
骓不逝兮可奈何，
虞兮虞兮奈若何！

作者简介

项羽（公元前232年—公元前202年），名籍，字羽，秦下相（今江苏宿迁）人，楚国名将项燕之孙。项羽生于乱世，少年勇武，心存大志。秦二世元年（公元前209年），项羽随叔父项梁在吴中（今江苏苏州）起义，杀伐征战，无敌天下。项梁战死后，他率军渡河救赵王歇；巨鹿之战，大败秦名将章邯。项羽金戈铁马，灭秦后，自封西楚霸王，后与刘邦楚汉相争。公元前202年，项羽兵败垓下（今安徽灵璧南），突围至乌江（今安徽和县长江段西）边，拔剑自刎。

古人评曰："羽之神勇，千古无二。"迄今为止，项羽一直被认为是中国冷兵器时代最为勇猛的武将。

4. Song of Gaixia

Qin Dynasty: Xiang Yu

My strength can pull hills up; O my spirit unrivaled in the world;
Times are going against me; O my black steed can gallop no more.
My black steed can gallop no more; O what should I do?
O Yu, O Yu, what can I do for you?

五、和垓下歌

秦朝：虞姬

汉兵已略地，
四方楚歌声。
大王意气尽，
贱妾何聊生？

作者简介

虞姬，名虞（一说姓虞），西楚霸王项羽的美人；相传有"虞美人"之称。

史书对虞姬本名、民族、出生地等均无记载。司马迁《史记·项羽本纪》仅记载："有美人名虞。"故出现两种观点：一则"虞"是美人的名；二则"虞"是美人的姓。《辞源》备有此说；"虞姬"则是后人对其称呼。"姬"也有两种说法：一则"姬"就是她的姓；二则"姬"是对古代妇女的美称。"虞姬"的"姬"为第二义。

后人据《垓下歌》，以及相传是虞姬所作的《和垓下歌》臆想，公元前202年，项羽兵败，虞姬在楚营内自刎，故有"霸王别姬"之传说。

此诗《史记》和《汉书》均未见收载。唐张守节《史记正义》从西汉陆贾所撰《楚汉春秋》中引录。宋王应麟《困学纪闻》卷十二《考史》认为此诗是中国最早的五言诗，但仍待证实。

5. Reply to King Xiang's Song

Qin Dynasty: Yu Ji

The Han army has conquered our land;
Around us, from their camps are songs of the Chu Kingdom.
My king's heroism has been exhausted;
Why should I live in shame?

六、大风歌

西汉：刘邦

大风起兮云飞扬，
威加海内兮归故乡，
安得猛士兮守四方！

作者简介

刘邦（公元前256年—公元前195年），楚国沛县丰邑中阳里（今江苏丰县）人，汉朝开国皇帝、政治家、战略家。汉民族和汉文化开拓者之一，其历史功绩不可磨灭。

刘邦出身农家，秦时任沛县泗水亭长，因释放刑徒，亡匿于芒砀山（今河南永城芒山镇）中。陈胜起事，刘邦响应，攻占沛县等地，称沛公，后投奔项梁，封武安侯。

公元前206年十月，刘邦驻军霸上（今白鹿原），秦王子婴投降。秦朝灭亡。刘邦废秦苛法，与关中父老约法三章。鸿门宴后封汉王，统治巴蜀及汉中一带。

刘邦知人善任，注意纳谏，终击败项羽，统一天下。公元前202年，刘邦即皇帝位，史称西汉。

汉朝初建，刘邦建章立制，崇尚"黄老之学""无为而治"，安抚民心，打下汉朝雍容大度的文化基础。他依法治国、刑德并用，是中国古代社会、政治管理者的典范。

6. Song of a Gale

Western Han Dynasty: Liu Bang

A gale is rising; O clouds are flying;

I have conquered the world; O I have come back to my hometown;

O how can I find warriors to guard the country's borders!

七、上邪

西汉：毛苹

上邪！
我欲与君相知，
长命无绝衰。
山无陵，
江水为竭，
冬雷震震，
夏雨雪，
天地合，
乃敢与君绝！

作者简介

毛苹，长沙王吴芮的妃子，史上著名才女，据传《上邪》是其作品。

公元前473年，勾践灭吴国，毙夫差；夫差子孙隐匿于今江西浮梁瑶里等偏僻之地。公元前248年，吴芮之父吴申被贬番邑（今鄱阳），后迁至余干县善乡龙山南麓（今社庚乡），吴芮出生于此，为夫差第十一世孙。

秦朝建立，吴芮任鄱邑令。陈胜起事，吴芮响应，后随项羽，封衡山王。

吴芮结识张良，改拥刘邦。公元前204年，吴芮取长沙，建古城。公元前202年初，吴芮受封为长沙王，低调行事，得善终。

公元前201年，吴芮与爱妻毛苹泛舟湘江，庆祝自己四十岁生日，毛苹吟咏《上邪》。同年，夫妻无疾而终，合葬长沙城西。

《上邪》极富浪漫主义色彩，爱情如岩浆喷发，激情逼人。明代胡应麟《诗薮》："《上邪》言情，短章中神品！"

7. O Heaven

Western Han Dynasty: Mao Ping

O Heaven!

I am dying to love you and be loved;

May our love, after a long life, still sparkle!

Only if mountains are flattened,

Only if rivers dry up,

Only if it thunders in winter,

Only if it snows in summer,

Only if the sky and the earth close up,

Dare I, with you, part!

八、龟虽寿

东汉：曹操

神龟虽寿，
犹有竟时。
螣蛇乘雾，
终为土灰。
老骥伏枥，
志在千里。
烈士暮年，
壮心不已。
盈缩之期，
不但在天。
养怡之福，
可得永年。
幸甚至哉，
歌以咏志。

作者简介

曹操（公元155年—公元220年），字孟德，小字阿瞒，沛国谯县（今安徽亳州）人。东汉末年政治家、军事家、文学家，三国时曹魏政权奠基人，即魏武帝。

曹操"挟天子以令诸侯"，对内灭袁氏、吕布等势力，对外降服南匈奴、乌桓、鲜卑等，统一中国北方，恢复生产和社会秩序，奠定了曹魏立国的基础。

曹操推行法治，抑制豪强，任人唯贤，政治清明，天下慕德，毛泽东曾言："曹操是了不起的政治家、军事家……"

曹操精兵法，著有《孙子略解》等书；善诗歌，《观沧海》等诗气魄雄伟，悲凉沉雄，有君临天下之气度。鲁迅称曹操"是一个改造文章的祖师"，认为其散文"清峻、通脱"，开启并繁荣了建安文学，史称"建安风骨"。

8. Though the Tortoise Enjoys Longevity

Eastern Han Dynasty: Cao Cao

Though the supernatural tortoise enjoys longevity,
Its life will end anyway.
Though the flying snake rides on clouds,
It will turn into ashes someday.
An old swift horse lies beside the manger,
And yet it dreams of a faraway place.
In old age, a man of heroic endeavor
Still dreams of running on to lead the race.
One's lifespan, whether long or short,
Is not just decided by Heaven.
Cultivation of one's body and spirit
Can help promote one's life extension.
I am such a lucky man;
I am singing to express my aspiration.

九、七步诗

东汉：曹植

煮豆燃豆萁，
豆在釜中泣。
本是同根生，
相煎何太急？

作者简介

曹植（公元192年—公元232年），字子建，沛国谯县（今安徽亳州）人。曹操之子，曹丕同母弟，受封陈王，谥号"思"，故称"陈思王"。

曹植是建安文学的代表人物，与曹操、曹丕合称"三曹"。钟嵘在中国第一部诗论《诗品》中认为，曹植之诗"源出于国风，骨气奇高，词采华茂，情兼雅怨，体被文质，粲溢今古，卓尔不群"。清朝诗人王士祯曾论，汉魏以来两千年间诗家堪称"仙才"者，曹植、李白、苏轼三人耳。

公元220年，曹丕称帝，曹植倍受迫害。曹丕病逝，其子曹叡对曹植继续高压。公元232年腊月，曹植抑郁而死。

9. A Poem Written in Seven Steps

Eastern Han Dynasty: Cao Zhi

Soybean stalks are burnt to cook pods;
Soybean pods are crying in the cauldron.
We were both born of the same root;
Why should you be so hard on me?

作者简介

陶渊明（公元 352 年或 365 年—公元 427 年），字元亮，又名潜，世称"靖节先生"。浔阳柴桑（今江西九江柴桑区）人。东晋末至南朝宋初期诗人、辞赋家，被称为"古今隐逸诗人之宗"。

陶渊明是中国第一位田园诗人，其诗纯朴自然、高远拔俗、情感深厚，影响了唐代田园诗派。苏东坡评曰："渊明诗初看似散缓，熟看有奇句。……大率才高意远，则所寓得其妙，造语精到之至，遂能如此。似大匠运斤，不见斧凿之痕。"

作为中国第一个大量写饮酒诗的诗人，他以"醉诗"批判是非颠倒的上流社会，反映仕途险恶，表现退出宦海的怡然自得，或困顿中的牢骚。鲁迅曾言：陶潜正因为并非浑身是"静穆"，所以他伟大。

陶渊明崇尚自然、真理、自由，傲岸不屈，人格高洁。《桃花源记》和《归去来兮辞》等辞赋最见其魏晋风度。

十、归园田居（其一）

魏晋：陶渊明

少无适俗韵，
性本爱丘山。
误落尘网中，
一去三十年。
羁鸟恋旧林，
池鱼思故渊。
开荒南野际，
守拙归园田。
方宅十余亩，
草屋八九间。
榆柳荫后檐，
桃李罗堂前。
暧暧远人村，
依依墟里烟。
狗吠深巷中，
鸡鸣桑树颠。
户庭无尘杂，
虚室有余闲。
久在樊笼里，
复得返自然。

10. Returning to Yuantianju Dwelling (1st Poem)

Wei & Jin Dynasties: Tao Yuanming

In childhood, I have not been used to everydayness;
I was born a nature lover.
I fell into the secular world due to carelessness;
It has been thirty years altogether.
A caged bird longs for its former forestland;
The pond fish yearns for its old pool deep.
I am reclaiming the southern wasteland;
Retiring from office, a simple rural life I keep.
Around my home, there is about two acres of land;
I have also eight or nine thatched cottages.
Elm and willow trees shade the back eaves, and
Before the rooms stand peach and plum trees.
In the distance, a village is vague and dim;
Over the village, smoke swirls softly upward.
From the deep lane several dog barks come;
From the tops of the mulberry trees roosters are heard.
The courtyard is clean and free from odds and ends;
My heart, free of preoccupations, is at its leisure.
Living so long a caged life, oh, my friends,
I finally return to nature.

十一、饮酒

魏晋：陶渊明

结庐在人境，
而无车马喧。
问君何能尔？
心远地自偏。
采菊东篱下，
悠然见南山。
山气日夕佳，
飞鸟相与还。
此中有真意，
欲辨已忘言。

11. Drinking

Wei & Jin Dynasties: Tao Yuanming

I built a humble house in a community,
Yet I am free of the hustle and bustle of the city.
How could I make it?
With a serene heart, I make my house detached.
While, at the east fence, picking chrysanthemum flowers,
Leisurely, I see, in the distance, the south mountains.
Mountain clouds and the setting sun are fantastic;
In pairs, birds are flying back.
In all these lies the way of the world;
I want to make it known, yet have forgotten the word.

作者简介

公元四世纪到公元六世纪，中国北方多为鲜卑、匈奴等少数民族统治，先后建立了北魏、北齐、北周等五个政权，史称"北朝"。

北朝民歌主要是北魏之后用汉语记录的作品。歌谣豪放刚健，质朴无华，体现了北方民族英勇豪迈的气概。史书中，最先提到《敕勒歌》[①]的是唐初李延寿撰的《北史》，最早见录于宋代郭茂倩所编《乐府诗集》之《杂歌谣辞》。

学者认为，这首民歌是由鲜卑语，或敕勒语，译成汉语，产生于公元五世纪中后期。全诗境界开阔，音调雄壮，艺术概括力极强；它是中国境内民族对抗与融合的历史见证，是中华文化形成进程中的典型个案，具有较高的文学、史学、文化学和民族学价值。

[①] 据唐朝初年李延寿所撰《北史》卷六《齐本记》：公元546年，北齐奠基人高欢率军十万，攻打西魏军事重镇玉壁（今山西南部稷山县西南），折兵七万。退兵晋阳途中，谣言起，传其中箭将亡。高欢带病设宴，强振军心，命部将斛律金唱《敕勒歌》。将士闻歌，军心大振。

译者注：据网络资料，今人大多只识此歌上半部，而下半部鲜为人知，不知其故！有观点认为，下半部是后人补作，非原文。本选本把下半部录入，供读者参考。个人认为，从"振军心"而言，下半部似乎更能使将士热血沸腾！

十二、敕勒歌

北朝民歌

敕勒川，
阴山下，
天似穹庐，
笼盖四野。
天苍苍，
野茫茫，
风吹草低见牛羊。

男儿血，
英雄色。
为我一呼，
江海回荡。
山寂寂，
水殇殇。
纵横奔突显锋芒。

12. Song of Chi'le Nationality

A Folk Song of the Northern Dynasties

The Chi'le grassland plain

Lies at the foot of the Yinshan Mountain.

The sky there looks like a dome,

Enveloping the wilderness to make a home.

The sky is bright blue;

The wilderness is beyond view;

The wind blowing, the grass bending, cattle and sheep appear.

A man's blood

Is the color of a hero.

Cry out for me aloud;

Rivers and seas echo.

Mountains are still;

Rivers rush and roll.

Charging east or west, a man shows his best in the fighting year.

作者简介

王勃（约公元650年—约公元675年），字子安，绛州龙门（今山西河津）人，与杨炯、卢照邻、骆宾王并称"初唐四杰"。公元675年或676年夏，自交趾（今越南）探望父亲北返，渡南海，不幸溺水而亡。

王勃善于五律和五绝，代表作有《送杜少府之任蜀州》等；其骈文成就之高，堪称一时之最，代表作为《滕王阁序》等。

王勃融儒、释、道于一身，主张仁政，希望济世；他鄙世傲物，处事疏阔；崇信佛教。他主张"立言见志"的文学思想，其诗文"高情壮思"，以雄壮著称。

十三、送杜少府之任蜀州

唐代：王勃

城阙辅三秦，
风烟望五津。
与君离别意，
同是宦游人。
海内存知己，
天涯若比邻。
无为在歧路，
儿女共沾巾。

13. To See Police Commissioner Du Off for Shuzhou City

Tang Dynasty: Wang Bo

The Three Qins area has protected Chang'an for many a generation.
In the mist, I gaze from afar at the five ferries at your destination.
Seeing you off, I find it hard to part,
Since we both serve in government.
Within the Four Seas, I am lucky to have you as my bosom friend;
We seem to live nearby, though we are at the earth's opposite end.
When we part at a fork in the road, there is no need
To wet the handkerchiefs, like young lovers, with tears shed.

作者简介

陈子昂（约公元661年—公元702年），字伯玉，梓州射洪（今四川射洪县）人。初唐诗文革新人物之一，曾任右拾遗（咨询建议官员，相当于监察兼助理），后世称为陈拾遗。

陈子昂具有政治见识和才能，敢谏言，但未被武则天采纳，屡受打击，心情郁愤。他登上幽州蓟北楼远望，悲从中来，感人生短促，天地悠悠。

《登幽州台歌》风格明朗刚健，具有"汉魏风骨"，是唐代诗歌的先驱之作。在艺术上，其意境雄浑，视野开阔；语言苍劲奔放，极富感染力；短短四句，展现了一幅境界雄浑、浩瀚空旷的艺术画面。

十四、登幽州台歌

唐代：陈子昂

前不见古人，
后不见来者。
念天地之悠悠，
独怆然而涕下。

14. Song of Ascending the You Prefecture Tower

Tang Dynasty: Chen Zi'ang

Before me, I cannot see the ancient wise king;
Behind me, I cannot see an intelligent monarch coming.
Thinking of the everlasting of sky and earth,
I cannot help feeling sorrowful, tears streaming down my face.

作者简介

张若虚（约公元660年—约公元720年），扬州（今江苏扬州）人；与贺知章、张旭、包融并称"吴中四士"。其诗细腻，音节和谐，清丽开阔，富有情韵，在初唐诗风的转变中有重要地位。《全唐诗》仅存张若虚之诗二首。

《春江花月夜》沿用陈朝（南陈）、隋朝乐府旧题。清末文学家王闿运评曰："孤篇横绝，竟为大家"；闻一多认为，在初唐宫体诗中，《春江花月夜》是"诗中的诗，顶峰上的顶峰"。

《春江花月夜》意境深邃，语言清新，韵律宛转，神韵深远。虽出自宫体，却全无脂粉之气，全诗展现的是一幅空灵纯美、情景交融、凄美自然的月夜春花流水图。

十五、春江花月夜

唐代：张若虚

春江潮水连海平，
海上明月共潮生。
滟滟随波千万里，
何处春江无月明！
江流宛转绕芳甸，
月照花林皆似霰；
空里流霜不觉飞，
汀上白沙看不见。
江天一色无纤尘，
皎皎空中孤月轮。
江畔何人初见月？
江月何年初照人？
人生代代无穷已，
江月年年只相似。
不知江月待何人，
但见长江送流水。
白云一片去悠悠，
青枫浦上不胜愁。
谁家今夜扁舟子？
何处相思明月楼？
可怜楼上月徘徊，
应照离人妆镜台。
玉户帘中卷不去，
捣衣砧上拂还来。

15. A Flower-and-Moon Night on the Spring River

Tang Dynasty: Zhang Ruoxu

Of the spring river, the tidewater is merging with the sea;

On the sea, the moon is rising with the tide simultaneously.

With the waves, for thousands of miles, the moonlight rolls away;

How can a spring river have no bright moon on such a day!

Through the meadows, the river zigzags, flowers fragrant at night;

Like ice pellets, the flowers glow under the moonlight.

In the air, the flying frost cannot be sensed;

On the beach, white sand cannot be distinguished.

The river shares the sky's color, no haze in between;

In the bright sky, only a lone moon is seen.

Who was the first one on the riverside to see the moon?

Which year did the moon in the river start to shine on man?

Generation after generation, life goes on and on;

Year after year, the moon in the river is always the same one.

I do not know for whom the moon in the river is waiting;

I only see the water in the Yangtze River keeps flowing.

A piece of white cloud floats leisurely across the sky;

At the Green Maple riverside, sorrow will never die.

Who is leaving home tonight in a small boat?

In which moonlit upstairs chamber does lovesickness float?

In the miserable upstairs chamber, the moon is lingering;

On the left-behind wife's dressing table it must be shining.

In jade chambers, moonlight on bead curtains cannot be pulled aside;

On the stone laundry slab, the flicked-off moonlight is back like a tide.

此时相望不相闻,
愿逐月华流照君。
鸿雁长飞光不度,
鱼龙潜跃水成文。
昨夜闲潭梦落花,
可怜春半不还家。
江水流春去欲尽,
江潭落月复西斜。
斜月沉沉藏海雾,
碣石潇湘无限路。
不知乘月几人归,
落月摇情满江树。

We long for each other now, but our voices cannot get through;

I wish to follow the moonlight to shine upon you.

Swan geese① can fly long, yet they cannot fly out of the moonlight;

Fish and Loong② swimming or jumping, only ripples are in sight.

Last night, in my dream, into a deserted pool flowers were falling;

Pitifully, spring days half gone, I have not begun my homecoming.

Spring is drifting in river water and about to disappear;

The moon in the riverside pool is again setting and drear.

The setting moon is hiding itself in the mist over the sea;

From Mount Jieshi to rivers Xiao and Xiang, so distant is the journey.

How many travellers are going home before the moon sets, I wonder;

The setting moon is arousing the feelings of rustling trees along the river.

---

① **swan goose:** a rare large goose with a natural breeding range in inland Mongolia, northernmost China, and southeastern Russia. It is migratory and winters mainly in central and eastern China. This species has been domesticated.
② **Loong:** mythical creatures portrayed in ancient Chinese, with head of a horse, horns of a deer, ears of cattle, body of a snake, scales of a carp, claws of a hawk, palms of a tiger, with whiskers and beard but no wings, capable of altering itself in size, length and color. It is highly mobile in water as well as among clouds. It is generally regarded as benevolent and the source of rain, thunder and lightning. Loong is spiritually linked to the Chinese and highly regarded as the Chinese nation symbol. Chinese are proud of being called "descendants of Loong." Apparently, Loong is misinterpreted as "dragon." In fact, Loong is so different in nature from the dragon that it is more reasonable to consider the two as unrelated creatures. Loong is also regarded as the symbol of luck, power, in particular, the Chinese emperors, so that they were called "the son of Loong."

十六、凉州词

唐代：王翰

葡萄美酒夜光杯，
欲饮琵琶马上催。
醉卧沙场君莫笑，
古来征战几人回。

作者简介

王翰（公元687年—公元726年），字子羽，并州晋阳（今山西太原）人，边塞诗人。

公元710年，王翰进士及第，直言极谏，仕途坎坷。他才智超群，举止豪放；杜甫曾发出"李邕求识面，王翰愿卜邻"的赞叹。

唐时，凉州（今甘肃武威）属陇右道；武则天时期，凉州、洛阳、扬州为唐朝三大经济中心。因与突厥、吐蕃相邻，凉州音乐多杂有西域龟兹（今新疆库车一带）之音。开元年间，陇右经略使郭知运把凉州曲谱进献唐玄宗，一时风行；众多诗人依曲谱创作《凉州歌》和《凉州词》。

王翰之诗情感奔放，最负盛名的是《凉州词》。此诗描绘了戍边将士置生死于度外的英雄气概；全诗语言精练，色彩浓郁，节奏明快。诗中，大唐将士豪迈之中带有一丝悲凉，恣意之余却又有几分无奈、悲壮。

16. Liangzhou Lyrics

Tang Dynasty: Wang Han

Good wine in luminous jade cups,

About to drink to pipa[①] music, we are urged to mount horses.

Laugh not at me if I get drunk and lie on the battlefield;

How many warriors ever returned from the wars of the world?

---

① **pipa:** a four-stringed Chinese musical instrument, belonging to the plucked category of instruments. Sometimes called the Chinese lute, the instrument has a pear-shaped wooden body with a varying number of frets ranging from 12 to 26.

作者简介

张九龄(公元678年—公元740年),字子寿,一名博物,谥"文献"。韶州曲江(今广东韶关市)人,世称"张曲江""文献公"。唐玄宗时名相;西汉留侯张良之后。

张九龄有远见,直言敢谏,刚正不阿,选贤任能,为"开元之治"作出了贡献,为后人所崇敬。他举止优雅,风度不凡,时人誉为"曲江风度"。张九龄去世后,唐玄宗对宰相推荐之士,总要问"风度得如九龄否?"

他提出以"王道"替代"霸道",强调保民育人,反对穷兵黩武;主张省刑罚,薄征徭,革新吏治。他主管开凿大庾岭路,此路成了南北交通要道,被后人誉为"古代的京广线"。

张九龄早年之诗词采清丽,情致深婉,晚年之诗朴素遒劲;其诗以兴为主,委婉蕴藉,兼有"风""骚"情韵。他追求诗歌的"象外之象、言外之意",独具"雅正冲淡"神韵。其诗《感遇》列《唐诗三百首》第一首。

继陈子昂之后,他力排齐梁颓风,追踪汉魏风骨,打开盛唐诗坛局面,对岭南诗派的开创和发展有深远影响。

十七、望月怀远

唐代:张九龄

海上生明月,
天涯共此时。
情人怨遥夜,
竟夕起相思。
灭烛怜光满,
披衣觉露滋。
不堪盈手赠,
还寝梦佳期。

17. Looking at the Moon and Cherishing the Faraway Place

Tang Dynasty: Zhang Jiuling

The bright moon is rising out of the sea;
Far apart, we share the moon's beauty.
Lovers hate the long and lonely night;
The whole night through, I miss you in the moonlight.
Blowing out the candle, I admire the full moon;
Putting on my coat, I feel the cold dew soon.
I cannot present you with my hands the moonlight;
I had better go and meet you in my dream tonight.

作者简介

孟浩然（公元689年—公元740年），名浩，字浩然，襄州襄阳（今湖北襄阳）人，世称孟襄阳，因未曾入仕，又称"孟山人"。孟浩然是盛唐山水田园诗派第一人，与王维并称"王孟"。

孟浩然诗歌的主题多为隐居闲适、羁旅愁思；其诗风清淡自然，恬适安静。其诗意境纯净，结构完美，情景交融，却又不事雕饰，尽得自然之美。孟浩然开启了中国山水诗创作新的篇章。在其诗中，诗人内心的情感、精神映射到物质世界的物象之上，使之和诗人心灵的颤动融为一体，从而获得生命、气质和神韵。《春晓》一诗如行云流水，自然浑成，而意境清迥，韵致流溢。

十八、宿建德江

唐代：孟浩然

移舟泊烟渚，
日暮客愁新。
野旷天低树，
江清月近人。

18. Staying Overnight on the Jiande River

Tang Dynasty: Meng Haoran

The boat has been punted to anchor by the islet misty;
The day darkening, a new sentiment is coming over me.
The wilderness extending away, the sky is lower than a tree;
The river is crystal clear and the moon is so close to me.

十九、春晓

唐代：孟浩然

春眠不觉晓，
处处闻啼鸟。
夜来风雨声，
花落知多少。

19. Spring Dawn

Tang Dynasty: Meng Haoran

Sleeping in spring, I know not dawn is arriving.
Here, there, and everywhere, I hear birds singing.
Last night, the wind was blowing, the rain falling,
How many flowers have fallen, I am wondering.

作者简介

王之涣（公元688年—公元742年），字季凌，绛州（今山西新绛县）人，盛唐著名诗人。据载，王之涣"慷慨有大略，倜傥有异才"，击剑悲歌，名动一时。与高适、王昌龄等人诗词唱和，善写边塞风光。

《清一统志》记载，鹳雀楼，又名鹳鹊楼，旧址在山西蒲州（今永济县）西南，黄河中高阜处，时有鹳雀栖其上，遂名。

《登鹳雀楼》开笔苍茫壮阔，气势雄浑，有"缩万里于咫尺，使咫尺有万里"之势。短短十字，上下空间转换，视觉近远位移，万里山河，尽收眼底；后两句把景物、哲理、情势融为一体，朴素深刻。诗忌说理，王之涣却能融理于景，融理于情；《登鹳雀楼》浑然天成，不愧为唐代五言诗的压卷之作！

二十、登鹳雀楼

唐代：王之涣

白日依山尽，
黄河入海流。
欲穷千里目，
更上一层楼。

20. Ascending the Stork Tower

Tang Dynasty: Wang Zhihuan

Behind the mountain, the sun is setting;
Towards the sea, the Yellow River is rolling.
If you want to enjoy the view to the fullest,
Ascend to another story, you must.

作者简介

贺知章(约公元659年—约公元744年),字季真,越州永兴(今浙江萧山)人;诗人,书法家。武则天证圣元年(公元695年)中乙未科状元,浙江历史上第一位有记载的状元。

贺知章旷达不羁,风流潇洒,为时人倾慕,有"清谈风流"之誉。其诗豪放,时人称之为"诗狂";与张若虚、张旭、包融并称"吴中四士";常与李白、张旭等饮酒赋诗,被称为"醉八仙";亦与陈子昂、李白、孟浩然、王维等结为"仙宗十友"。晚年放荡不羁,自号"四明狂客"。

贺知章诗文精佳,写景、抒怀之作风格独特,清新潇洒。其书法品位颇高,擅草隶。他读到李白之诗,赞"谪仙人也",并把李白引荐给唐玄宗。八十六岁,他告老还乡,旋逝。

二十一、回乡偶书(其一)

唐代:贺知章

少小离家老大回,
乡音无改鬓毛衰。
儿童相见不相识,
笑问客从何处来。

21. A Chance Writing When Returning to My Hometown (1st Poem)

Tang Dynasty: He Zhizhang

Leaving my hometown young, I returned at an old age.
My temples are grey; my accent has no change.
Meeting me, children know not who I am;
They smilingly ask me where I have come from.

二十二、回乡偶书（其二）

唐代：贺知章

离别家乡岁月多，
近来人事半消磨。
惟有门前镜湖水，
春风不改旧时波。

22. A Chance Writing When Returning to My Hometown (2nd Poem)

Tang Dynasty: He Zhizhang

I have been away from my hometown for many years;
In recent years, there have been so many changes.
Only the Mirror Lake before my old house remains the same;
In the spring breeze, ripples spread across as once they came.

二十三、黄鹤楼

唐代：崔颢

昔人已乘黄鹤去，
此地空余黄鹤楼。
黄鹤一去不复返，
白云千载空悠悠。
晴川历历汉阳树，
芳草萋萋鹦鹉洲。
日暮乡关何处是，
烟波江上使人愁。

作者简介

崔颢（公元704年—公元754年），汴州（今河南开封）人，公元723年中进士；早期之诗多以"闺情"为主。唐玄宗之时，杨氏弄权，人多敢怒不敢言，崔颢秉性耿直，书写诗文，针砭时弊、讽刺杨氏；后赴边塞，此后之诗，风骨凛然，慷慨豪迈，雄浑自然。

黄鹤楼原址在武昌蛇山黄鹄矶头，始建于公元223年。唐代《元和郡县图志》记载：孙权始筑夏口故城，"城西临大江，江南角因矶为楼，名黄鹤楼"。据考证，因建在黄鹄山上，在古代，"鹄"与"鹤"互为通用，故名"黄鹤楼"。

公元765年，黄鹤楼已具规模；历代名士到此吟诗作赋。崔颢《黄鹤楼》一诗，使其闻名遐迩，据说李白因之搁笔；1927年，毛泽东写下《菩萨蛮·登黄鹤楼》。

黄鹤楼屡毁屡建，最后一次被毁于1884年。1957年建长江大桥武昌引桥时，旧址被占，1981年黄鹤楼重建，选址在距旧址约1 000米的蛇山峰岭。1985年6月落成，主楼以清同治楼为蓝本。

23. The Yellow Crane Tower

Tang Dynasty: Cui Hao

Riding on a yellow crane, the immortal has left for years;
Right in this place, only the empty Yellow Crane Tower remains.
The yellow crane has gone, never to return;
For thousands of years, white clouds continue to float in vain.
In the bright sun, in the Hanyang Plain, trees are seen clearly;
On the Parrot Isle, grass grows lushly and luxuriantly.
The sun is setting, and where is my hometown?
Mist and waves on the Yangtze River let a heart down.

作者简介

王昌龄（公元698年—公元757年），字少伯，河东晋阳（今山西太原）人，又一说为长安（今西安）人。其诗以七绝见长，后人誉之为"七绝圣手"。据认为，王昌龄是边塞诗的先驱，七绝至王昌龄而体制大定。三十岁进士及第前，他以边塞诗著称。

王昌龄诗绪密而思清，语言精练，意蕴无穷。他善于捕捉典型情景，诗歌意境开阔，语言圆润蕴藉，音调婉转和谐，耐人寻味，在发情、造景、写意等方面均有很高造诣。

他提出"诗有三境"："一曰物境，二曰情境，三曰意境。"他反对意、景分离："若一向言意，诗中不妙及无味。景语若多，与意相兼不紧，虽理通亦无味"；重视情、景结合："凡诗，物色兼意下为好。若有物色，无意兴，虽巧亦无处用之。"

二十四、出塞

唐代：王昌龄

秦时明月汉时关，
万里长征人未还。
但使龙城飞将在，
不教胡马度阴山。

24. Out of the Frontier Fortress

Tang Dynasty: Wang Changling

The Qin Dynasty's moon is shining over the Han Dynasty's fortress;
The army has not returned from the long march and harshness.
If only General Li Guang from the Loong City were still alive,
The Hun horses could never cross the Yinshan Mountains and survive.

作者简介

王维（公元701年或公元699年——公元761年），字摩诘，号摩诘居士。河东蒲州（今山西运城）人。公元731年，王维状元及第；官至尚书右丞，世称"王右丞"。

王维精通诗、书、画、音乐等；与孟浩然合称"王孟"，有"诗佛"之称。王维书画特臻其妙，后人推其为南宗山水画之祖。苏轼评价："味摩诘之诗，诗中有画；观摩诘之画，画中有诗。"

王维写景清新自然，淡远之境自见，大有陶潜遗风。他扩大了山水诗的内容，使山水诗达到了前所未有的高度，其影响深远。

王维以画入诗，其山水诗层次丰富，远近相宜，动静相兼，声色俱佳，更多一层动感和音乐美；其诗歌语言含蓄，清新明快，句式、节奏富于变化，音韵和谐，具有音乐美；有些诗则清冷幽邃，充满禅意，山水意境已超出自然美学，进入宗教境界。

二十五、山居秋暝

唐代：王维

空山新雨后，
天气晚来秋。
明月松间照，
清泉石上流。
竹喧归浣女，
莲动下渔舟。
随意春芳歇，
王孙自可留。

25. An Autumn Evening in the Mountain Village

Tang Dynasty: Wang Wei

In the empty mountain, fresh rain has stopped;
The weather in the autumn evening is pleasant.
The bright moon is shining upon the pine trees;
Crystal spring water is flowing down over stones.
In the bamboo, lasses are heard to return from clothes washing;
Lotus leaves wavering, a fishing boat is out there net casting.
Even though spring flowers have faded away,
In the village, I am perfectly willing to stay.

二十六、鹿柴

唐代：王维

空山不见人，
但闻人语响。
返景入深林，
复照青苔上。

26. Stick Fence for Deer

Tang Dynasty: Wang Wei

In the empty mountain no man is seen,
But human voices are heard in the forest green.
Sun rays reflected by clouds penetrate through deep trees,
And shine again upon moss in the evening breeze.

二十七、相思

唐代：王维

红豆生南国，
春来发几枝。
愿君多采撷，
此物最相思。

27. Lovesickness

Tang Dynasty: Wang Wei

Jumby beans grow in the south of China;
In springtime, new twigs come out every year.
May you collect more when seeds ripen!
They are the very thing for lovesickness.

二十八、送元二使安西

唐代：王维

渭城朝雨浥轻尘，
客舍青青柳色新。
劝君更尽一杯酒，
西出阳关无故人。

欣赏笔记

28. To See Yuan'er Off as an Envoy to An'xi

Tang Dynasty: Wang Wei

Morning rain in Weicheng city moistened the dust;
The inn is cloaked in spring, willows freshly green.
Please, my friend, drink one more cup of wine;
Leaving the Yangguan Pass, you will meet no old friends out west.

作者简介

李白（公元701年—公元762年），字太白，号青莲居士，又号"谪仙人"；被后人誉为"诗仙"，与杜甫并称"李杜"。

李白的籍贯、出生地尚无定论，主要有以下观点：1.唐剑南道绵州昌隆（今四川绵阳江油市青莲场）；2.陇西成纪（今甘肃天水市秦安县叶堡乡）；3.出生于安西都护府碎叶城（今吉尔吉斯斯坦的托克马克市），四岁随父迁绵州昌隆县。

李白家世，在唐代就讳莫如深，其祖父、曾祖父，史料无一记载。《旧唐书》记载，李白之父李客为任城尉。李白鲜谈家世，偶有所及，闪烁其辞。

《新唐书》记载，李白为兴圣皇帝（凉武昭王李暠）九世孙。依此说，李白与李唐诸王同宗，是唐太宗李世民同辈族弟；亦有说其是李建成玄孙。

公元742年，因贺知章举荐，唐玄宗召见李白，令其供奉翰林。李白反对唐玄宗好大喜功，穷兵黩武，后遭谗谤。公元755年，安史之乱爆发，李白入永王李璘府为幕僚，怂恿李璘称帝；永王败北，李白流放夜郎（即今贵州一带）。公元759年，获赦；公元762年，病逝（李白之死有三种说法：醉死、病死、溺死）。

在乐府、歌行及绝句创作方面，李白的歌行打破了诗歌固有格式，空无依傍，笔法多样，变幻莫测。其绝句自然明快，飘逸潇洒，情思无尽。在盛唐诗人中，兼长五绝与七绝，且同臻极境的，唯李白一人；其诗歌影响深远。李白的诗雄奇飘逸，意境奇妙，想象奇特，富有浪漫主义精神，达到了内容与艺术的完美统一，有"笔落惊风雨，诗成泣鬼神"的艺术魅力。李白常将想象、夸张、比喻等修辞综合运用，从而造成神奇、瑰丽的意境。

在词体文本模式的形成、词的创作模式上，李白之词具有开创意义。

二十九、月下独酌（其一）

唐代：李白

花间一壶酒，
独酌无相亲。
举杯邀明月，
对影成三人。
月既不解饮，
影徒随我身。
暂伴月将影，
行乐须及春。
我歌月徘徊，
我舞影零乱。
醒时相交欢，
醉后各分散。
永结无情游，
相期邈云汉。

29. Drinking Alone under the Moon (1st Poem)

Tang Dynasty: Li Bai

A jug of wine in the flowers,

I am drinking alone, without the company of dear ones.

Holding my cup, I invite the bright moon for a drink;

There are altogether three of us, including my shadow.

The moon never understands the wonder of taking a drink;

The shadow, in vain, follows me from head to toe.

For the moment, the moon and the shadow keep me company;

In such a beautiful spring night, I will eat, drink and be merry.

While I am singing, the moon is journeying;

While I am dancing, the wild shadow is following.

Awake, we enjoy each other's company;

Drunk, we are parted and go on our own journey.

I hope we can be emotionless travel companions forever,

And meet in the boundless Milky Way to wander.

三十、月下独酌（其二）

唐代：李白

天若不爱酒，
酒星不在天。
地若不爱酒，
地应无酒泉。
天地既爱酒，
爱酒不愧天。
已闻清比圣，
复道浊如贤。
贤圣既已饮，
何必求神仙。
三杯通大道，
一斗合自然。
但得酒中趣，
勿为醒者传。

30. Drinking Alone under the Moon (2nd Poem)

Tang Dynasty: Li Bai

If Heaven does not love wine,

The god of wine① should not be in Heaven.

If Earth does not love wine,

The Wine Spring② should not be on Earth.

Since both Heaven and Earth love wine,

My love of wine does not make me unworthy of Heaven.

I heard that crystal wine was compared to a saint;

I was also told that turbid wine was regarded as a sage.

Since both the saint and the sage drink wine,

Why should we worship immortal deities?

Three cups of wine can help reach the Great Way;

Drinking a bucket of wine perfectly match with nature.

I care only about the wonder of having a drink,

And tell not those who are wide-awake.

---

① **god of wine:** (in ancient Chinese astronomy) the name of a star in the sky, also called the wine banner star.
② **the Wine Spring:** (*jiuquan* in Chinese Pinyin) the Wine Spring Prefecture (Jiuquan Prefecture) in the Han Dynasty in Chinese history. It was said that in the prefecture there was a spring, and the taste of water in the spring was like wine, so the spring was named the Wine Spring. It is now in Jiuquan city in Gansu Province.

三十一、行路难

唐代：李白

金樽清酒斗十千，
玉盘珍羞直万钱。
停杯投箸不能食，
拔剑四顾心茫然。
欲渡黄河冰塞川，
将登太行雪满山。
闲来垂钓碧溪上，
忽复乘舟梦日边。
行路难！
行路难！
多歧路，
今安在？
长风破浪会有时，
直挂云帆济沧海。

31. Hard Is the Journey

Tang Dynasty: Li Bai

Good wine in golden vessels costs one thousand taels[①] per gallon;
Delicacies in jade dishes are worth ten thousand taels altogether.
Putting down my cup and chopsticks, I suddenly lost my appetite;
Pulling out the sword and looking around, I feel at a loss and bitter.
I want to sail across the Yellow River, but it is still frozen;
I intend to climb the Taihang Mountains and they are yet snow-clad.
Unoccupied, Lü Shang[②] went fishing in the Wei River in the sun;
Suddenly, Yi Yin[③] dreamt of sailing past the sun after he retired.
Hard is the journey!
Hard is the journey!
On the road, too many forks are there;
Where is my destination?
A time will come when I sail downwind in waves and walk on air;
Raising the sail high, I will fearlessly voyage the great ocean.

[①] **tael:** any of the various units of weight used in eastern Asia, roughly equivalent to 38 grams ($1\frac{1}{3}$ ounces), also a unit of currency formerly used in China, equivalent in value to this weight of standard silver.

[②] **Lü Shang:** the clan name of Jiang Ziya, who was an ancient Chinese general and lived around the 8th century BC. He is famous for his role in overthrowing the last emperor of the Shang Dynasty. Having previously served under the emperor, Lü Shang had grown to hate him. Being an expert in military strategy and affairs, he decided to wait until the time was right to strike. Only when somebody sought him out and recognized his talents would he help overthrow the emperor. He retired to the Wei River and spent his days calmly fishing. He had an unusual style of fishing, and he fished using a barbless hook. He fished without a hook believing that the fish would bite of their own free will when the time was right and that to a patient person, a hook would not be needed. When Lü Shang turned 80 years old, his unusual style of fishing reached the ears of King Wen. King Wen first sent a soldier and then an official to bring Lü Shang to him, but they were both refused, being told that Lü Shang would wait for a larger fish to bite. Finally, King Wen went himself to speak with Lü Shang and greeted him courteously, he asked: "Do you take pleasure in fishing?" Lü Shang replied: "Man of true worth takes pleasure in realizing his ambitions; the common man takes pleasure in doing his best for his affairs. My fishing is very much like it." Being impressed with his answer, King Wen took Lü Shang into his service.

[③] **Yi Yin:** a minister of the early Shang Dynasty. He was one of the most honored officials of the early Shang Dynasty. He helped Tang of Shang, the founder of the Shang Dynasty, to defeat King Jie of Xia. Oracle inscriptions of Yi Yin have been found, and the evidence shows that his social status was high. During the early Shang Dynasty, Yi Yin helped Tang set up different institutions, resulting in stability in politics as well as economic benefits.

三十二、登金陵凤凰台

唐代：李白

凤凰台上凤凰游，
凤去台空江自流。
吴宫花草埋幽径，
晋代衣冠成古丘。
三山半落青天外，
二水中分白鹭洲。
总为浮云能蔽日，
长安不见使人愁。

32. Ascending the Phoenix Terrace of Nanjing

Tang Dynasty: Li Bai

Auspicious phoenixes visited the Phoenix Terrace in history;
The phoenixes gone, the terrace empty, the Yangtze flows ceaselessly.
Flowers of the King of Wu's Palace grow in secluded lanes all around.
The cenotaph of Guo Pu of the Eastern Jin is now an ancient mound.
The Sanshan Hill is far away under the blue skies;
The Egret Isle splits the Qinhuai River into two waterways.
Floating clouds and treacherous court officials hide the sun from view;
Chang'an, the capital city, is beyond my reach and makes me blue.

三十三、早发白帝城

唐代：李白

朝辞白帝彩云间，
千里江陵一日还。
两岸猿声啼不住，
轻舟已过万重山。

33. Leaving Baidi City in Early Morning

Tang Dynasty: Li Bai

In early morning, in colorful clouds I bid farewell to Baidi City;
In a day, I will be back in a thousand-li-away Jiangling County.
Along the two banks of the Yangtze River gibbons are heard;
Thousands of mountains the sampan boat has already passed.

三十四、静夜思

唐代：李白

床前明月光，
疑是地上霜。
举头望明月，
低头思故乡。

34. Thoughts on a Still Night

Tang Dynasty: Li Bai

Around the well is bright moonlight;
It might be frost on the ground, I suspect at night.
Looking up at the bright moon high in the sky,
And lowering my head, I miss my hometown and sigh.

三十五、赠汪伦

唐代：李白

李白乘舟将欲行，
忽闻岸上踏歌声。
桃花潭水深千尺，
不及汪伦送我情。

35. To Wang Lun for Seeing Me Off

Tang Dynasty: Li Bai

Li Bai, in a boat, is departing;
Suddenly I hear singing ashore accompanied by dancing.
The Peach Flower Pool is a thousand feet deep,
Yet, it is not as deep as Wang Lun's friendship.

作者简介

常建（公元708年—?），邢州（今河北邢台，据墓碑记载）人。公元727年，与王昌龄同榜进士，且有文字相酬。常建官场失意，耿介自守，交游无显贵。在唐代殷璠的选本《河岳英灵集》中，常建位于卷首，在李白、王维等人之前。在序言中，殷璠对其不吝赞誉之词。

常建之诗意境清迥，语言洗练自然，独具一格。其诗以山水田园为主，风格接近"王孟"。他善于运用凝练简洁的笔触，表达清寂幽邃的意境。唐代山水诗多歌咏隐逸情趣，常建《题破山寺后禅院》一诗优游自得，禅宗佛音如天籁之音，深邃超脱。

三十六、题破山寺后禅院

唐代：常建

清晨入古寺，
初日照高林。
曲径通幽处，
禅房花木深。
山光悦鸟性，
潭影空人心。
万籁此俱寂，
惟余钟磬音。

36. About the Buddhist Retreat behind the Poshan Temple

Tang Dynasty: Chang Jian

In early morning, I entered the ancient temple;
The rising sun shone upon tall mountain trees.
A winding lane stretched to a place peaceful;
Buddhist living quarters hid behind lush flowers.
The mountain scenery excited the singing birds;
My heart was emptied by the reflection in the pool.
Right here, all the sounds have faded into silence;
I hear only the voice of chime and bell.

作者简介

杜甫（公元712年—公元770年），字子美，自号少陵野老；巩县（今河南巩义）人。与李白合称"李杜"；后世称其杜拾遗、杜工部、杜少陵、杜草堂，和"诗圣"；其诗被称为"诗史"。

杜甫远祖为汉武帝时著名酷吏杜周，祖父杜审言（唐代"近体诗"奠基人之一）。杜甫与"小李杜"的杜牧同为晋代大学者、名将杜预之后。

公元744年四月，杜甫与李白相遇洛阳；四年后，两人再会兖州，寻仙访道，谈诗论文。杜甫哀国难，叹民苦；曾为官数载，因痛心时政，放弃官职。在严武的帮助下，杜甫在成都建成一座草堂，世称"杜甫草堂"。公元770年冬，杜甫在一条小船上去世。

杜甫之诗沉郁顿挫，其诗多涉笔政治黑暗、社会动荡、人民疾苦，以及唐朝由盛转衰的巨变；其作品被称为世上疮痍。杜甫的诗歌对中国文学和日本文学产生了深远影响。

鲁迅曾言："我总觉得陶潜站得稍稍远一点，李白站得稍稍高一点，这也是时代使然。杜甫似乎不是古人，就好像今天还活在我们堆里似的，"又云"杜甫是中华民族的脊梁！"

三十七、春望

唐代：杜甫

国破山河在，
城春草木深。
感时花溅泪，
恨别鸟惊心。
烽火连三月，
家书抵万金。
白头搔更短，
浑欲不胜簪。

37. A Glimpse in Spring

Tang Dynasty: Du Fu

The capital occupied, rivers and mountains are yet the same;
In the city, wild grass is lush and green after spring came.
Saddened and grieved, my tears splashed onto flower petals;
Departing from my family, at the birds' chirping my heart trembles.
For three months, flames and smoke of war endured;
As ten thousand taels of gold is a family letter counted.
My gray head I scratch and thinner my hair is getting;
It can hardly be held together with a clasp as it is thinning.

三十八、登高

唐代：杜甫

风急天高猿啸哀，
渚清沙白鸟飞回。
无边落木萧萧下，
不尽长江滚滚来。
万里悲秋常作客，
百年多病独登台。
艰难苦恨繁霜鬓，
潦倒新停浊酒杯。

38. Ascending High

Tang Dynasty: Du Fu

The wind sudden and strong, the sky is high, apes tragically crying;
The islet desolate, the sand beach deserted, birds are migrating.
Countless leaves, rustling and rustling, are falling;
The endless Yangtze, rolling and rolling, is flowing.
For thousands of miles, in chilly autumn, I travelled to many a place;
One hundred years old, illness-stricken, I ascend alone the terrace.
Hardships and bitterness have dyed my temples gray;
Poverty-stricken, I stopped raising the wine cup the other day.

三十九、春夜喜雨

唐代：杜甫

好雨知时节，
当春乃发生。
随风潜入夜，
润物细无声。
野径云俱黑，
江船火独明。
晓看红湿处，
花重锦官城。

欣赏笔记

39. A Good Rain in the Spring Night

Tang Dynasty: Du Fu

A good rain knows the season;
When spring comes, it falls then.
Following the wind, it slipped into the night,
And voicelessly moistened plants like moonlight.
Paths in the field have been shrouded by the dark cloud;
Only lights on the river boats flickered in the wind.
Tomorrow, at dawn, I will look at the red and wet flower;
They must make Chengdu city a sea of glamour.

四十、蜀相

唐代：杜甫

丞相祠堂何处寻？
锦官城外柏森森。
映阶碧草自春色，
隔叶黄鹂空好音。
三顾频烦天下计，
两朝开济老臣心。
出师未捷身先死，
长使英雄泪满襟。

40. The Chancellor of the Kingdom of Shu[①]

Tang Dynasty: Du Fu

Where can I find the Wuhou Temple[②]?
It is outside Chengdu city where cypress trees are lush and tall.
Grass between stone steps alone makes the spring;
Blocked by leaves, an oriole, in vain, is heard beautifully singing.
Liu Bei visited Zhuge's thatched cottage thrice for current affairs;
In building the Kingdom, he whole heartedly served two rulers.
Launching unsuccessful military expeditions, he died for the mission,
Reducing heroes to tears that their clothes dampen.

---

① **The Chancellor of the Kingdom of Shu:** namely Zhuge Liang, courtesy name Kongming, a Chinese politician, military strategist, writer, engineer and inventor. He served as the chancellor and regent of the state of Shu Han during the Three Kingdoms Period. He is admired and recognized as the most accomplished strategist of his era.
② **Wuhou Temple**, also known as Wuhou Shrine, or Wuhou Memorial Temple, or Memorial Temple of Marquis Wu, is dedicated to Zhuge Liang, the Marquis Wu (Wuhou) of the Kingdom of Shu in the Three Kingdoms Period (AD 220–280) in Chinese history. Zhuge Liang was the personification of noble character and intelligence. Memorial architectures erected in many places after his death include a famous one in Chengdu.

作者简介

岑参（约公元715年—公元770年），荆州江陵（现湖北江陵）人，太宗功臣岑文本重孙，早岁孤贫，从兄就读，遍览史籍。唐玄宗天宝三年（公元744年）进士，曾任嘉州（今四川乐山）刺史，世称"岑嘉州"。

岑参善七言歌行，风格与高适相近，并称"高岑"。盛唐诗人中，其边塞诗数量最多，成就最为突出。

岑参早期诗歌多写景、述怀；其写景诗清丽隽永、"语奇体峻，意亦造奇"（殷璠《河岳英灵集》）。岑参中年两次出塞，诗歌风格大变，开拓了边塞诗的题材和艺术境界。其诗作充满奇情异彩，诗风沉雄淡远，意境新奇，雄奇瑰丽，富有浪漫主义色彩。岑参晚年入蜀，其山水诗奇丽新奇，"随物赋形"，思想趋于隐逸。

陆游曾称赞说，"以为太白、子美之后一人而已"。

四十一、白雪歌送武判官归京

唐代：岑参

北风卷地白草折，
胡天八月即飞雪。
忽如一夜春风来，
千树万树梨花开。
散入珠帘湿罗幕，
狐裘不暖锦衾薄。
将军角弓不得控，
都护铁衣冷难着。
瀚海阑干百丈冰，
愁云惨淡万里凝。
中军置酒饮归客，
胡琴琵琶与羌笛。
纷纷暮雪下辕门，
风掣红旗冻不翻。
轮台东门送君去，
去时雪满天山路。
山回路转不见君，
雪上空留马行处。

41. Song of Snow on Seeing the Aide Mr. Wu Off for the Capital

Tang Dynasty: Cen Shen

The north wind swept across the land, white grass bending;

In the eighth lunar month, from the barbarian sky, snow was falling.

Just as overnight, the spring breeze has arrived,

And thousands of pear trees have blossomed.

Snowflakes flew through the bead curtain, wetting the tent within;

The fox fur coat could not warm, the silk brocade quilt too thin.

Frozen, the generals' horn bows could not be drawn;

The frontier officers' armor was too cold to put on.

The vast desert has been ice-coated and lifeless;

Downcast dark clouds were endless and motionless.

In the commander's tent, a banquet was held for the leaving aide;

The instruments, huqin[①], pipa and qiang flute[②], were played.

Snow was pouring down outside the camp gate;

The wind blowing, the red flag was frozen and straight.

I saw you off at the east gate of Luntai town;

Then, snow covered the roads of Tianshan Mountain.

The path winding and turning, you were no more to be seen;

In vain, horse trails were there, leaving the snow white and clean.

[①] **huqin:** any of a group of Chinese fiddles. Huqin are generally spike fiddles, as the narrow cylindrical or hexagonal body is skewered by the tubular neck. Most have two strings, although some three- or four-string variants exist. The instruments are held vertically on the player's lap, and their music is marked by slides and vibrators as the left hand moves quite freely along the strings. Typically, the horsehair of the bow passes between the strings and the arched wooden stick remains on the outside; the bow is thus not separable from the instrument.

[②] **qiang flute:** an ancient single-reed gas singing instrument in China. It has a history of more than 2,000 years. It is popular in the Qiang people's residence of Aba Tibetan Autonomous Prefecture in northern Sichuan.

四十二、渔歌子

唐代：张志和

西塞山前白鹭飞，
桃花流水鳜鱼肥。
青箬笠，
绿蓑衣，
斜风细雨不须归。

作者简介

张志和（公元732年—公元810年？），字子同，初名龟龄，婺州（今浙江金华）人，自号"烟波钓徒"，又号"玄真子"。

张志和十六岁参加科举，以明经擢第，因才华出众，受唐肃宗李亨赏识，赐名"志和"。"安史之乱"使其思想和处世趋于消极；因事获罪贬南浦（今重庆万州），不久赦还。母亲和妻子相继故去。感于宦海风波、人生无常，遂弃官离家，浪迹江湖，隐居祁门赤山镇。

唐肃宗曾赐他奴婢各一人，张志和让他们结婚，取名渔童和樵青。他常去水滨河溪，效法姜太公无饵垂鱼。

公元810年秋冬，颜真卿游览平望驿，张志和酒酣耳热，飘然若仙，乘兴表演水上游戏。颜真卿为他撰碑铭说：张志和自沉于水。

42. Song of the Fisherman

Tang Dynasty: Zhang Zhihe

Before the Xisai Mountain, egrets are flying;

In the water, mandarin fish is fat, peach flowers floating.

With a cyan bamboo hat,

And a green sedge raincoat,

Amid the breeze and the drizzle, I need not go back.

作者简介

张继（约公元715年—约公元779年），字懿孙，襄州（今湖北襄阳）人。约公元753年中进士，与刘长卿、皇甫冉交好。其诗爽朗激越，不事雕琢，比兴幽深，事理双切，对后世颇有影响。

寒山寺是日本人心目中的文化圣地；清朝国学大师俞樾在《新修寒山寺记》写道："凡日本文墨之士咸造庐来见，见则注注言及寒山寺，且言其国三尺之童，无不能诵是诗者。"《枫桥夜泊》和寒山寺已经成了中日交流的文化符号。

日本在东京也建造了寒山寺，且刻了《枫桥夜泊》诗碑。1905年，日本赠送一口"仿唐青铜乳头钟"给寒山寺，钟上铭文为汉字，乃时任首相伊藤博文所书。钟一式两口，另一口在日本馆山寺。

唐代以来，诗僧寒山逐渐成了日本的文化偶像，其名声远胜其他诗人，因寒山之诗充满了对生命无常的体验与顿悟，其人生观与诗的意境和日本的民族特点极其吻合。

四十三、枫桥夜泊

唐代：张继

月落乌啼霜满天，
江枫渔火对愁眠。
姑苏城外寒山寺，
夜半钟声到客船。

43. Anchoring at Night by Maple Bridge

Tang Dynasty: Zhang Ji

The moon set, ravens cawing, frost occupied the sky;
Facing maple leaves and fishing boat lights, I sleep in melancholy.
Outside Gusu city, from Hanshan Temple,
Tolls of the midnight bell spread to the traveler vessel.

作者简介

刘长卿（约公元726年—约公元786年），字文房，宣州（今安徽宣城）人。唐玄宗天宝进士，官至随州刺史，世称刘随州。刘长卿善于五言，自称"五言长城"。

刘长卿的诗含蓄蕴藉，兴在象外。他善于用白描手法对景物做细致描写，但他取于物象，而又不滞于物象。其诗篇有如画面，意蕴深远，令人心旷神怡，回味无穷。他能够以情写景、借景抒情，达到情景交融、浑然一体的艺术境界。

清代沈德潜曾言刘长卿之诗"工于铸意，巧不伤雅，犹有前辈体段也"。

四十四、逢雪宿芙蓉山主人

唐代：刘长卿

日暮苍山远，
天寒白屋贫。
柴门闻犬吠，
风雪夜归人。

44. The Host in Whose House I Lodge on a Snowy Day on the Confederate Rose Mountain

Tang Dynasty: Liu Changqing

At dusk, green mountains seem far away;
The thatched cottage is shabby on such a cold day.
A dog is heard barking from the stick gate;
He is returning on the windy and snowy night.

作者简介

孟郊（公元751年—公元815年），字东野，湖州武康（今浙江德清县）人；有"诗囚"之称，与贾岛齐名，人称"郊寒岛瘦"。

孟郊四十六岁才中进士，未能施展抱负，遂放迹山水。他清寒终身，耿介倔强。

孟郊之诗多关于世态炎凉、民间疾苦。透过个人卑微的命运，他以诗来反映纷繁的社会生活，针砭社会丑恶和贫富不均。

孟郊诗风古朴凝重，新奇别致；其词采险奇艰涩，精思苦吟；其诗情深致婉，气势磅礴；为韩愈推崇，成为韩愈诗派名士。

闻一多曾评价："从中国诗歌的整体发展过程着眼，最能结合自己生活实践，继承发扬杜甫写实精神，为写实诗歌继续向前发展开出一条新路的，似乎应该是终身苦吟的孟东野。"

四十五、游子吟

唐代：孟郊

慈母手中线，
游子身上衣。
临行密密缝，
意恐迟迟归。
谁言寸草心，
报得三春晖。

45. Song of the Traveling Son

Tang Dynasty: Meng Jiao

A needle and thread in my loving mother's hand,
She is sewing for her son leaving for a faraway land.
Before my departure, she is stitching the clothing carefully,
Afraid I might return later than scheduled unexpectedly.
Who said that the tiny heart of grass
Could repay the sun's love and kindness?

四十六、慈母吟

唐代：孟郊

时梦返故园，
庭院草木侵。
痛不见慈颜，
长留带泪吟。
慈亲养育我，
眷眷鞠劳心。
耕作一何苦，
持家一何殷。
教诲严有道，
仁义秉忠勤。
为人须良善，
读书惜寸阴。
但求业有就，
非图步青云。
懿德尊为鉴，
遗言作家训。
平生当奋力，
不负慈母心。

46. Song of My Loving Mother

Tang Dynasty: Meng Jiao

I dreamt of returning to my hometown;
In the yard, wild grass was lushly green.
I was heartbroken for not seeing my mother;
Weeping, for a long time I sighed there.
My loving mother reared me;
She brought me up devotedly.
How industrious she was in farming!
How considerate she was in housekeeping!
In rearing me, she was ingenious and strict.
She was gentle, righteous, loyal and diligent.
"A man must be good and kind;
Value each minute to become educated and refined;
I only hope that you get established in society,
Not that you become a high-ranking official quickly."
I will hold your virtue up as an admonition,
And pass your words on to future generations.
All my life I should make arduous efforts,
And never fail to meet my loving mother's expectations.

作者简介

柳宗元（公元773年—公元819年），字子厚，河东（今山西芮城、运城一带）人，唐宋八大家之一，文学家、哲学家、散文家和思想家，世称"柳河东""河东先生"，因官终柳州刺史，又称"柳柳州"。柳宗元与韩愈并称"韩柳"，与刘禹锡并称"刘柳"，与王维、孟浩然、韦应物并称"王孟韦柳"。

柳宗元二十一岁进士及第，成为革新派重要人物；公元805年，"永贞革新"失败，柳宗元被贬为邵州刺史，后加贬为永州司马。公元815年三月，他被改贬为柳州刺史；十一月，因病去世，仅四十七岁。元和十年，柳宗元写下《永州八记》等317篇诗文。

柳宗元推崇"古文"运动，其散文论说性强，讽刺辛辣；其哲学、政论等杂文，笔锋犀利，论证精确；其寓言发展了《庄子》等传统，抨击社会丑恶现象，善用动物形象，表现了高度的讽刺艺术；其山水游记以永州之作为胜，借景寄寓遭遇和怨愤，抒发苦难中的精神寄托；其诗词骚赋独具特色，深得楚辞精髓。

柳宗元把古代朴素唯物主义无神论思想发展到了一个新的高度，是中唐杰出的思想家。毛泽东评价说："柳宗元是一位唯物主义哲学家……"

四十七、江雪

唐代：柳宗元

千山鸟飞绝，
万径人踪灭。
孤舟蓑笠翁，
独钓寒江雪。

47. River Snow

Tang Dynasty: Liu Zongyuan

Birds are not heard on thousands of mountains,
People are not seen on millions of paths.
A coir raincoat and a bamboo hat on, an elder, in a boat,
Is fishing alone, on a cold river, in the snow white.

作者简介

张籍(约公元766年—约公元830年),字文昌,和州乌江(今安徽和县乌江镇)人,世称"张水部""张司业"。张籍为韩愈大弟子,公元799年进士及第;其乐府诗与王建齐名,并称"张王乐府"。

张籍倡导新乐府运动,其乐府诗多反映社会现实和矛盾,同情民众疾苦。张籍的乐府诗成就斐然。他善于概括事物对立面,在数篇或一篇之中形成强烈对比。他还善用素描手法,细致真实地刻画人物形象。

其诗语言凝练、平易自然,而又峭炼含蓄,常以口语入诗。他着意提炼结语,达到意在言外的批判和讽刺效果。张籍的五律,不事藻饰,不假雕琢,于平易流畅中见委婉深挚,对晚唐五律影响较大。

四十八、节妇吟·寄东平李司空师道

唐代：张籍

君知妾有夫,
赠妾双明珠。
感君缠绵意,
系在红罗襦。
妾家高楼连苑起,
良人执戟明光里。
知君用心如日月,
事夫誓拟同生死。
还君明珠双泪垂,
恨不相逢未嫁时。

48. Ode to a Chaste Wife · To Minister Li Shidao of Dongping

Tang Dynasty: Zhang Ji

You know I have been married already,
Yet, a bright pair of pearls you presented me.
To express my gratitude for your lingering longing,
I attached them to my red upper silk garment with a string.
Our high edifices are next to the royal garden, and
My husband is an Imperial guard with a halberd in his hand.
I know your intentions are like the sun and the moon in the sky,
I have yet vowed to keep my husband company till I die.
I returned you the bright pearls, my tears streaming down;
How I hate not to have met you before putting on my bridal gown.

作者简介

元稹(公元779年—公元831年),字微之,别字威明,河南洛阳人。北魏宗室鲜卑拓跋部后裔,北魏昭成帝拓跋什翼犍十九世孙。公元793年,元稹明经及第,曾一度拜相,然宦海浮沉,四度被贬。公元831年,元稹去世,白居易为其撰写了墓志。

唐德宗贞元九年(公元793年),十五岁的元稹以明两经擢第。唐代科举名目甚多,而报考最多的科目则为进士和明经两科。不过两科相比也有难易之分,进士科难,"大抵千人得第者百一二";明经科"倍之,得第者使一二",故有"三十老明经,五十少进士"之说,而唐代文人也更为看重进士科。元稹为尽快摆脱贫困,获取功名,选择投考的为相对容易的明经科,一战告捷。及第之初的元稹却一直无官,闲居于京城。但他没有终止勤奋学习。家庭藏书给他提供了博览群书的条件,京城的文化环境和他的广泛兴趣,陶冶了他的文化修养。次年得陈子昂《感遇》诗及杜甫诗数百首悉心读之,始大量作诗。贞元十五年(公元799年),二十一岁的元稹寓居蒲州,初仕于河中府。此时,正当驻军骚乱,蒲州不宁。元稹借助友人之力保护处于危难之中的远亲。乱定,与其家少女相爱。不久,元稹牵于功名,西归京城应制科试。元稹才华出众,性格豪爽,奉职勤恳,一心为民。他大胆劾奏不法官吏,平反冤案,得到民众的崇高赞誉。

元稹与白居易同科及第,结为终生诗友,共同倡导新乐府运动,世称"元白",形成"元和体"。其乐府诗创作受到张籍、王建影响,"新题乐府"直接缘于李绅。

元稹诗文兼擅;其诗最具特色的是艳诗和悼亡诗,他擅写男女爱情,描述细致生动,铺叙详密,优美自然。元稹推崇杜甫之诗,其诗平浅明快,色彩浓烈,细节刻画真切动人。

四十九、离思

唐代:元稹

曾经沧海难为水,
除却巫山不是云。
取次花丛懒回顾,
半缘修道半缘君。

49. Thought after Departing

Tang Dynasty: Yuan Zhen

Having seen the great sea, I know no greater waters;
Having been to the Wushan Mountains, I know no better clouds.
Walking past flowers, I have no desire to cast my eyes on them;
I do this in part practicing Taoism and in part for you, my madam.

作者简介

刘禹锡（公元772年—公元842年），字梦得，洛阳人；先祖为汉景帝贾夫人之子中山靖王刘胜。刘禹锡与柳宗元并称"刘柳"，与韦应物、白居易合称"三杰"，与白居易合称"刘白"；有"诗豪"之称。

公元793年，刘禹锡与柳宗元同榜进士及第，成为革新集团核心人物。因革新失败屡遭打击，但他始终不屈，一生历任多职。

刘禹锡的山水诗景象开阔疏朗，具有超强的时空感。因性格刚毅，其诗风独特，多简洁明快，风情俊爽。其诗融诗人的真挚与哲人的睿智为一体，极富艺术张力。

刘禹锡的哲学思想具有鲜明的唯物主义倾向。刘禹锡认为，自然界充满了有形的物质实体，天地之内不存在无形的东西。他批驳玄学、佛教和道教关于"空""无"是宇宙本原的理论，认为"空"是一种特殊的物质形态，不能超越物质形体而独立存在。这是中国古代唯物主义自然观的重大发展。

五十、陋室铭

唐代：刘禹锡

山不在高，
有仙则名。
水不在深，
有龙则灵。
斯是陋室，
惟吾德馨。
苔痕上阶绿，
草色入帘青。
谈笑有鸿儒，
往来无白丁。
可以调素琴，
阅金经。
无丝竹之乱耳，
无案牍之劳形。
南阳诸葛庐，
西蜀子云亭。
孔子云：何陋之有？

50. An Epigraph on the Simple House

Tang Dynasty: Liu Yuxi

The height of a mountain matters not;

With an immortal, it becomes great.

The depth of waters matters not;

With a Loong, it is blessed.

Though the house is simple,

I am a man of character noble.

Up on stone steps crept marks of moss green;

Through the bamboo curtain, lush grass is seen.

Here, great scholars are chatting and laughing;

Among my guests, nobody is a know-nothing.

I can play the unadorned qin,

And read gold-dust-written Buddhist Scriptures within.

No disturbing noises come from the string or the pipe instrument;

No physical pain arises from office desk work of the government.

In Nanyang is the thatched cottage once lived in by Zhuge Liang;

In western Shu there is the pavilion formerly lodged by Yang Xiong[1].

Confucius once said: "How can it be said to be simple?"[2]

---

[1] **Yang Xiong:** a poet and writer, born in Chengdu in Shu Prefecture in the Western Han Dynasty (53 BC–AD 18).
[2] Confucius once wanted to move to a remote place to live. However, someone said: "That place is too simple, and what should we do?" Hearing that, Confucius said: "When a gentleman lives there, how can it be said to be simple?"

作者简介

白居易（公元772年—公元846年），字乐天，号香山居士，祖籍太原，生于河南新郑，唐代三大诗人之一；有"诗魔"和"诗王"之称。

公元802年，与元稹同科进士及第，成为挚友，共同倡导新乐府运动。诗坛齐名，世称"元白"。

他不畏权贵，上书论事，被贬江州（今江西九江）司马。贬谪江州是其一生转折点，其思想从"兼济天下"转向"独善其身"，常与刘禹锡唱和，时称"刘白"。

其诗歌题材广泛，语言优美、通俗，音调和谐，形象鲜明，以讽喻诗和闲适诗为主。讽喻诗志在"兼济"，与社会政治紧相关联，意激气烈；闲适诗意在"独善"，"知足保和，吟玩性情"（《与元九书》）。他善用白描勾勒人物形象，以浅白之句寄托讽喻之意，得怵目惊心之艺术效果。

白居易提出了"文章合为时而著，歌诗合为事而作"的现实主义创作原则。

五十一、琵琶行

唐代：白居易

浔阳江头夜送客，
枫叶荻花秋瑟瑟。
主人下马客在船，
举酒欲饮无管弦。
醉不成欢惨将别，
别时茫茫江浸月。
忽闻水上琵琶声，
主人忘归客不发。
寻声暗问弹者谁？
琵琶声停欲语迟。
移船相近邀相见，
添酒回灯重开宴。
千呼万唤始出来，
犹抱琵琶半遮面。
转轴拨弦三两声，
未成曲调先有情。
弦弦掩抑声声思，
似诉平生不得志。
低眉信手续续弹，
说尽心中无限事。
轻拢慢捻抹复挑，
初为《霓裳》后《六幺》。
大弦嘈嘈如急雨，
小弦切切如私语。
嘈嘈切切错杂弹，
大珠小珠落玉盘。
间关莺语花底滑，
幽咽泉流冰下难。

51. Song of Pipa

Tang Dynasty: Bai Juyi

At the riverside of the Xunyang River, I saw a guest off at night;
Maple leaves and silver grass flowers rustled in autumn moonlight.
The guest and I dismounted from our horses and boarded the boat;
We raised cups to drink without music from pipe or string instrument.
Getting drunk, yet cheerless, we were sad and about to part;
Parting, we saw the vast darkness and the moon on the river bright.
Suddenly, we heard the sound of the pipa coming from the water;
I forgot to return, the guest having no desire to leave the harbor.
Locating the sound source, I asked in the darkness who was playing;
The pipa music stopped for a while, no one replying.
We moved our boat closer to hers, inviting her for a get-together;
Filling up the cups, we made the oil lamp brighter for another dinner.
Invited over and over again, she finally appeared from the cabin;
She held a pipa, behind it half of her face hidin'.
Twice or thrice, she turned the turning peg and plucked the strings;
Before a tune was played, her gestures expressed her inner feelings.
Each string was miserable, each tone thoughtful;
The tune seemed to be speaking of her life unsuccessful.
Lowering her eyebrows, she randomly played the pipa without stop;
In her music, she told endless stories in her heart from the top.
Light squeezing, slow rubbing, pulling, backhand pulling twice,
She played firstly *Fairy's Clothes* and then *Liu Yao* music nice.
The sound of the heavy string was like a sudden shower;
The sound of the light string seems like a soft whisper.
The heavy and sudden sound interwove with the one light and sedate;
They were like big or small pearls falling onto the plate.
The music was soft and smooth, like orioles in flowers chirping;
The sound was then like water under ice, intermittent and whispering.

欣赏笔记

冰泉冷涩弦凝绝,
凝绝不通声暂歇。
别有幽愁暗恨生,
此时无声胜有声。
银瓶乍破水浆迸,
铁骑突出刀枪鸣。
曲终收拨当心画,
四弦一声如裂帛。
东船西舫悄无言,
唯见江心秋月白。
沉吟放拨插弦中,
整顿衣裳起敛容。
自言本是京城女,
家在虾蟆陵下住。
十三学得琵琶成,
名属教坊第一部。
曲罢曾教善才服,
妆成每被秋娘妒。
五陵年少争缠头,
一曲红绡不知数。
钿头银篦击节碎,
血色罗裙翻酒污。
今年欢笑复明年,
秋月春风等闲度。
弟走从军阿姨死,
暮去朝来颜色故。
门前冷落鞍马稀,
老大嫁作商人妇。
商人重利轻别离,
前月浮梁买茶去。

The ice-cold water was motionless as if the strings were frozen;

It stopped flowing and the music died all of a sudden.

It seemed a hidden sorrow and hatred was sprouting;

Silence now, than a voice, was more moving.

Suddenly, a sound, like a silver bottle, crashed, water scattering;

It sounded like swords and spears striking and a cavalry dashing.

A tune over, with a plectrum, she plucked the middle as ever:

Like tearing cloth, the four strings sounded altogether.

People in the boats around kept still;

In the middle of the river, the white moon was seen in autumn chill.

Pondering, between the strings she inserted the plectrum;

Straightening her clothes, she looked solemn.

She claimed to have been born in the capital city;

At the foot of Hamaling her family used to be.

She had learned to play the pipa at the age of thirteen;

In the Music Bureau, she was listed as a top-tier musician.

A tune finished, she was admired by music masters;

Make-up done, she was envied by other courtesans.

Rich young men in the capital vied to give her gifts;

Finishing a tune, she was given countless bolts of red silk fabric.

Gold jewels and silver double-edged combs used to beat time broke;

Her red and thin silk skirt was stained with the wine of the young folk.

One year after another, she spent her life having fun;

In autumn moonlight and spring wind, she wasted her life's seasons.

Her brother joined the army and her mother died;

Dusk going and dawn coming, her golden age over, she aged.

Few horses and carriages came to her desolate house;

Her youth vanishing, she married and was a merchant's spouse.

Valuing profits over love, the merchant was on a business trip;

Last month, he went to Fuliang to buy tea in a ship.

欣赏笔记

去来江口守空船，
绕船月明江水寒。
夜深忽梦少年事，
梦啼妆泪红阑干。
我闻琵琶已叹息，
又闻此语重唧唧。
同是天涯沦落人，
相逢何必曾相识！
我从去年辞帝京，
谪居卧病浔阳城。
浔阳地僻无音乐，
终岁不闻丝竹声。
住近湓江地低湿，
黄芦苦竹绕宅生。
其间旦暮闻何物？
杜鹃啼血猿哀鸣。
春江花朝秋月夜，
往往取酒还独倾。
岂无山歌与村笛？
呕哑嘲哳难为听。
今夜闻君琵琶语，
如听仙乐耳暂明。
莫辞更坐弹一曲，
为君翻作《琵琶行》。
感我此言良久立，
却坐促弦弦转急。
凄凄不似向前声，
满座重闻皆掩泣。
座中泣下谁最多？
江州司马青衫湿。

He left and she was alone to stay on the empty boat;

Around the boat, the water was cold and the moonlight bright.

In the dead of night she dreamt of her early days;

She cried in the dream and all over her face were tear stains.

Hearing the pipa, I sighed;

Hearing her life story, I again sighed.

We were both drifters in the world;

Before our meeting, we did not need to be acquainted.

Last year, I left the capital city;

Demoted and sick, I lived in Xunyang city.

In remote Xunyang city, there is no music;

All year long, I hear no pipe or string music or a single lyric.

I live near the low-lying and humid Penjiang River;

Around my house, Amur barberries and bitter bamboos prosper;

What can be heard in the morning or in the evening?

Cuckoos are chirping till they bleed, apes tragically crying.

When flowers bloomed in spring or the Mid-Autumn moon shone,

Very often, I took the wine and drank alone.

Is not there folksong or village flute?

They are too crude and coarse to suit.

Tonight, through the pipa, I heard your feelings;

I seem to have heard celestial music with temporarily acute hearing.

Decline not to be seated to play another tune;

I will write you a new Song of Pipa at such a moment opportune.

Moved by me, she stood there for quite a while in the boat;

Back to her seat, she turned the strings tighter for the quick note.

The mournful tune differed from what she had just finished playing;

Hearing the music, all the people present covered their faces weeping.

Whose eyes of those present have cried the most tears?

I have wet my cyan robe, the uniform for Chancellor of Wars.

作者简介

崔护(公元772年—公元846年),字殷功,博陵(今河北定州)人,生平事迹不详。公元796年,进士及第。公元829年,为京兆尹(首都地区最高行政长官),同年为御史大夫、广南节度使。

崔护诗风精练婉丽,语极清新。《全唐诗》存诗六首,皆为佳作。《题都城南庄》以"人面桃花,物是人非"道出天下人的人生体验。崔护因一诗而不朽。

五十二、题都城南庄

唐代:崔护

去年今日此门中,
人面桃花相映红。
人面不知何处去,
桃花依旧笑春风。

52. A Poem on a Southern Village in the Capital City

Tang Dynasty: Cui Hu

This day last year, right inside this very gate,
A face and peach flowers were shining upon each other.
Now, the face is nowhere to be found on the estate;
The peach flowers are smiling in the spring breeze as ever.

作者简介

杜牧（公元803年—约公元852年），字牧之，号樊川居士，京兆万年（今陕西西安）人。宰相杜佑之孙，因晚年居长安南樊川别墅，后世称"杜樊川"。与李商隐并称"小李杜"。

杜牧博通经史，才华出众，专注治乱与军事；公元828年，杜牧进士及第，一生为官，兴利除弊，关心民众。

杜牧诗歌以七言绝句著称，咏史抒怀，英发俊爽，多切经世之物，在晚唐成就颇高，人称"小杜"，以别于"大杜"杜甫。

杜牧主张文以意为主，以气为辅，以辞采章句为兵卫。其古体诗受杜甫、韩愈影响，善于将叙事、议论、抒情融为一体，题材广阔，笔力峭健；其近体诗文词清丽、情韵跌宕。

清人沈德潜认为，杜牧绝句"托兴幽微"，可谓盛唐绝句之"嗣响"。

五十三、江南春

唐代：杜牧

千里莺啼绿映红，
水村山郭酒旗风。
南朝四百八十寺，
多少楼台烟雨中。

53. Spring in Regions South of the Yangtze River

Tang Dynasty: Du Mu

Thousands of miles around, orioles are singing, flowers blooming;
In waterside villages and hillside towns, tavern banners[①] are fluttering.
On the hundreds of Buddhist temples built in the Southern Dynasty,
Countless towers and terraces are bathed in rain misty.

---

① **a tavern banner:** a cloth flag hung outside a tavern in ancient China to attract customers. It is the oldest kind of advertisement in China and enjoys a long history. Traditionally, the Chinese character "wine" is written on the flag to show that wine is available in the tavern. A tavern banner is still in use today in some taverns in China to attract customers.

五十四、清明

唐代：杜牧

清明时节雨纷纷，
路上行人欲断魂。
借问酒家何处有？
牧童遥指杏花村。

54. Tomb Sweeping Day

Tang Dynasty: Du Mu

On Tomb Sweeping Day, it rains without a break;
Passersby are on a road of heartache.
I asked where I could find a tavern;
The shepherd boy pointed afar in Apricot Hamlet's direction.

作者简介

李商隐（约公元813年—约公元858年），字义山，号玉溪（谿）生，荥阳（今河南荥阳）人。

李商隐乃唐代皇族远房宗室，少时丧父，家境贫寒，成年后性格忧郁、敏感、清高。公元837年，李商隐进士及第；因卷入"牛李党争"，仕途坎坷。

李商隐追求诗美，"唐"所罕见；和杜牧合称"小李杜"；与李贺、李白合称"三李"；又与温庭筠合称"温李"，因与段成式、温庭筠诗文风格相近，且三人在家族里排行均为第十六，故并称"三十六体"。

李商隐的咏史诗借古讽今；其爱情诗缠绵悱恻，字字血泪，令人不忍卒读；其无题诗风格独特，多以爱情为题，意境"朦胧"，情思宛转，声调和美，隐晦迷离。

其近体诗继承了杜甫七律的沉郁顿挫，又融合了齐梁诗的浓艳、李贺之诗的奇幻、象征，形成了深情绵邈、绮丽精工的独特风格，是唐代七律发展史上的第二座丰碑。

李商隐是晚唐最重要的骈体文作家。范文澜认为，只要其《樊南文集》存留，唐代的骈体文就算全部遗失也不可惜。

五十五、锦瑟

唐代：李商隐

锦瑟无端五十弦，
一弦一柱思华年。
庄生晓梦迷蝴蝶，
望帝春心托杜鹃。
沧海月明珠有泪，
蓝田日暖玉生烟。
此情可待成追忆？
只是当时已惘然。

55. The Painted Se

Tang Dynasty: Li Shangyin

The painted se, for no reason at all, has fifty strings[①];

A string or a turning pin reminds me of our sweet years.

Zhuangzi dreamt of becoming a butterfly fluttering its wings[②];

King Wangdi shifted on to the cuckoo his bitter remorse[③].

The moon bright, sea pearls come from Chinese mermaids' tears[④];

The sun warm, from the jade in Lantian Mountain the mist is rising[⑤].

Why should I wait to brood over it after so many years?

At that time, I had already felt frustrated about parting.

---

① In the Tang Dynasty, the Chinese musical instrument se had twenty-five strings. In the poem, the poet Li Shangyin said that for no reason at all, the painted se had fifty strings, indicating that each string had broken into two, so altogether there were fifty strings. It is believed that Li Shangyin wrote the poem in the later years of his life, and then his wife had been dead for some years. In Chinese, "*Duanxian* (the broken string)" represents "the death of one's wife."

② Once Zhuang Zhou dreamt of becoming a butterfly that flitted about and fluttered around, and the butterfly was so happy and pleased, forgetting that he was Zhuang Zhou. Suddenly he woke up, and felt very agitated for a while. He finally realized that he was Zhuang Zhou himself. Was it that Zhuang Zhou had become a butterfly in his dream or a butterfly dreamt that it had become Zhuang Zhou? There must be some distinction between Zhuang Zhou and a butterfly. This is called the transformation between self and things. (Zhuangzi. *The Complete Works of Zhuangzi*. Guizhou: Guizhou People's Publishing House.)

③ In the ancient kingdom of Shu (now, Sichuan Province), King Wangdi, whose name was Du Yu, was a responsible and diligent king. Later, he abdicated the throne and lived a secluded life. Unfortunately, the kingdom was conquered, and he died of sorrow. After his death, his soul became a bird. When late spring came each year, the bird cuckooed till it bled from its mouth. Its blood dripped onto the mountains and changed into beautiful flowers. People were moved, and they named the bird cuckoo and the flowers azaleas.

④ According to a legend, in the South China Sea, there were Chinese mermaids (jiaoren in Chinese Pinyin), who lived like fish in water. They were very good at weaving, and when they cried, their tears became pearls.

⑤ Lantian Mountain in Shaanxi Province in China was famous for producing Lantian jade. Ancient people believed that when the sun was warm, the mist from jade would rise and float over Lantian Mountain. People could see the mist from afar, but when they got close to the Mountain, the mist was nowhere to be seen.

五十六、夜雨寄北

唐代：李商隐

君问归期未有期，
巴山夜雨涨秋池。
何当共剪西窗烛，
却话巴山夜雨时。

56. A Poem Written in the Night Rain to My Wife in the North

Tang Dynasty: Li Shangyin

You asked me the date for my return, but I still do not know;
In the Daba Mountains, the night rain has filled up the autumn ponds.
When can we together trim the wick by the western window?
I will tell you my feelings on the rainy night in the Daba Mountains.

五十七、铜官窑瓷器题诗

唐代：佚名

君生我未生，
我生君已老。
君恨我生迟，
我恨君生早。

作者简介

《铜官窑瓷器题诗》，即《铜官窑瓷器题诗二十一首》，是唐代民间五言诗歌。1974—1978年，题诗出土于湖南长沙唐代铜官窑窑址。

一般认为，题诗产生于"安史之乱"后，是中唐新兴的市民文学；诗由瓷工创作，或收录，题于所造瓷器之上。

题诗以写实为主，朴实无华，采用了"赋、比、兴"的创作手法，内容涉及相思、征战、宗教、商贾、游子、旅人等。

57. A Poem Inscribed on Porcelain from Tongguan Kiln

Tang Dynasty: Anonymous

When you were born, I have not yet come into the world.
When I was born, you have become old.
You hate me for coming late;
I hate you for being born too early to be my mate.

作者简介

李煜(公元937年—公元978年),字重光,号钟隐、莲峰居士,祖籍彭城(今江苏涂州铜山区),南唐最后一位国君,世称南唐后主、李后主。

李煜工书善画、能诗善词、通音晓津。他继承了花间派词人传统,语言明快,形象生动,用情真挚,风格鲜明,在晚唐五代词中别树一帜,对后世影响深远。

李煜之词,以亡国为界,分前、后两期:前期词旖旎柔情,尽述宫闱之乐,在人物、场景描写上艺术概括力强;后期词题材广阔,哀亡国之痛,悲婉凄凉,意境深远,极富艺术感染力。

李煜对词主要有以下贡献:1.扩大了词的表现领域,使词成为言怀述志的新诗体,对宋代豪放派词有影响;2.词境优美,感情纯真,审视人生悲剧,把个人遭遇泛化,赋予普遍意义;3.语言自然、精练,富有表现力和概括性;4.在风格上有独创性。

五十八、虞美人·春花秋月何时了?

北宋:李煜

春花秋月何时了?
往事知多少。
小楼昨夜又东风,
故国不堪回首月明中。

雕栏玉砌应犹在,
只是朱颜改。
问君能有几多愁?
恰似一江春水向东流。

58. Tune to "Beauty Yu" · When Will Spring Flowers and Autumn Moon End This Year?

Northern Song Dynasty: Li Yu

When will spring flowers and autumn moon end this year?
About how many memories are left I am not clear.
Last night, in my little upstairs chamber a vernal wind was blowing;
How could I bear missing my lost kingdom with the moon shining?

Carved railings and jade stairs must still be there;
They must be the same except for the ladies fair.
How many sorrows can you have, gentleman?
Just like spring water in the Yangtze, they flow eastward to the ocean.

五十九、相见欢·无言独上西楼

北宋：李煜

无言独上西楼，
月如钩。
寂寞梧桐深院锁清秋。
剪不断，
理还乱，
是离愁。
别是一般滋味在心头。

59. Tune to "A Happy Meeting"·Silent and Alone, Up the West Tower I Climb

Northern Song Dynasty: Li Yu

Silent and alone, up the west tower I climb;

The moon resembles a hook.

The deep courtyard locks the lonely phoenix tree and the late autumn.

I cut my sorrow with a pair of scissors, but it does not break;

I try to order it, but it remains a mess;

Parting sorrow it is.

Deep in my heart, it is yet another taste.

作者简介

范仲淹（公元989年—1052年），字希文，苏州吴县人。北宋杰出的思想家、政治家、文学家。

范仲淹幼年丧父，先祖是唐朝宰相范履冰。1015年，他苦读及第，历任多职，因秉公直言，屡遭贬斥。1027年，范仲淹守母丧，受晏殊之邀，执教应天书院。他创导时事政论，严以律己、崇尚品德，书院学风焕然一新。

1040年，范仲淹挂帅戍边，采取"屯田久守"策略，团结少数民族，巩固西北边防。1043年，他任参知政事，发起"庆历新政"，澄清吏治，改革科举等，是王安石"熙宁变法"前奏。新政失败，他被贬出京；1052年，病逝于上任颍州途中；谥号"文正"，世称范文正公。

他大力兴学，培养人才；晚年设义田，建义学，免费教育家族子弟，开启中国古代免费教育新风尚。

范仲淹认为，文章关系国家兴衰，反对柔靡文风，提出"宗经复古"，革新宋初文风。他主张诗歌忠于现实，不为空言。其诗意淳语清，以文为诗，重议论，善白描。范仲淹词作仅五首存世，在宋词的发展中承前启后；其《渔家傲·秋思》乃边塞词首创，影响了宋代豪放词和爱国词。

苏轼评曰：出为名相，处为名贤；乐在人后，忧在人先。经天纬地，阙谥宜然，贤哉斯诣，轶后空前。

六十、苏幕遮·怀旧

北宋：范仲淹

碧云天，
黄叶地，
秋色连波，
波上寒烟翠。
山映斜阳天接水，
芳草无情，
更在斜阳外。

黯乡魂，
追旅思，
夜夜除非，
好梦留人睡。
明月高楼休独倚，
酒入愁肠，
化作相思雨。

60. Tune to "The Head Scarf"·Nostalgia

Northern Song Dynasty: Fan Zhongyan

Clouds float across an azure sky;

Yellow leaves on the ground drift by;

Autumn scene mirrored in the water, waves roll away;

Over the waves, the cold mist is emerald in autumn day.

Mountains bathed in the setting sun, the sky is merging with the river;

Fragrant grass is unfeeling and makes me bitter;

Beyond the setting sun, the grass extends farther and farther.

Missing my hometown, I feel dejected;

My sorrows as a traveler cannot be dispelled;

Only if each night,

Good dreams come to make my sleep right.

When the moon shines upon the tower, do not lean alone on the railing;

Filled with sorrow, wine I am drinking;

The rain of lovesickness each cup is becoming.

作者简介

柳永（约公元984年—约1053年），原名三变，字景庄，后改名柳永，字耆卿，福建崇安人，北宋婉约词派代表人物。

柳永生于官宦世家，少有志于功名，后流寓苏、杭，科举四次落第，遂专心治词。1034年，柳永暮年及第，官至屯田员外郎（相当于国家粮食局副局长），世称柳屯田。柳永抚民勤政，被称为"名宦"。

柳永堪称北宋前期第一词家，他改旧腔，创新调，上承敦煌，下启金、元，创、用词调竟达一百五十之多，为两宋第一人。柳永之词以长调慢词为主，大部分词调前所未闻。

柳永善用俗词俚语，以北宋都市男、女情感和市井风情为主题，创作了大量平民化、大众化的词作。其词情真意切，旖旎风流，令人肝肠寸断，且雅俗共赏，对宋词发展影响深远。

六十一、雨霖铃·寒蝉凄切

北宋：柳永

寒蝉凄切，
对长亭晚，
骤雨初歇。
都门帐饮无绪，
留恋处，
兰舟催发。
执手相看泪眼，
竟无语凝噎。
念去去，
千里烟波，
暮霭沉沉楚天阔。

多情自古伤离别，
更那堪，
冷落清秋节！
今宵酒醒何处？
杨柳岸，
晓风残月。
此去经年，
应是良辰好景虚设。
便纵有千种风情，
更与何人说？

61. Tune to "Bells Ringing in the Rain"·Cicadas Are Mournfully Chirping

Northern Song Dynasty: Liu Yong

Cicadas are mournfully chirping;
In late evening, the pavilion we are facing;
A heavy shower just stopped.
Outside the capital gate, drinking in a tent, our hearts are dropped.
When we are unwilling to part,
The boat is urging me to depart.
Hand in hand, we look at each other through tearful eyes;
Unexpectedly, choking up, we are lost for words.
At the thought of the long journey ahead,
I see, for thousands of miles, mist-covered waters spread;
Evening clouds and mists low, the southern skies outspread.

Sentimentalists always feel heartbroken about departure;
How can they bear the torture
Of a bleak and cold autumn day!
Where do I, after sobering up tonight, lie?
By the riverside where weeping willows grow,
Under the waning moon when dawn breezes blow.
After the departure, for many years to come,
So trivial a sweet time or a beautiful scene must become.
Even if floods of love pour from my heart,
Who can I talk to without my sweetheart?

作者简介

晏殊（公元991年—1055年），字同叔，抚州临川县文港乡（今南昌市进贤县文港镇）人。北宋著名文学家、政治家。

晏殊五岁能文，十四岁入试，得宋真宗嘉赏，赐同进士出身。晏殊性格刚烈，不怒自威，但为人质朴，待人以诚；他富贵一生，却生活简朴；仕途偶有波澜，却长期身居要职，官拜宰相。1055年，病逝于汴京（今河南开封），封临淄公，谥号元献，世称晏元献。

晏殊唯贤是举，范仲淹、王安石皆出其门；他提携韩琦、富弼、欧阳修等，举荐良才，总领"庆历新政"。

晏殊重视教育。任职地方时，他支持书院发展，培养人才；任宰相时，与范仲淹倡导、开创州、县立学，革新教学内容，官学设教授。自此，从京师至郡县，均设有官学，史称"庆历兴学"。欧阳修曾说"自五代以来，天下学废，兴自公始"。

晏殊能诗，尤善小令，有"宰相词人"之称。他吸收了"花间派"和冯延巳的典雅词风，开创了北宋婉约词派，被称为"北宋倚声家之初祖"。其词音韵柔美、辞藻华美，风格含蓄婉丽，言富贵而不俗，情艳而不淫。无论闲雅、旷达，语言都清新自然、和谐圆润。与其子晏几道，称为"大晏"和"小晏"，与欧阳修并称"晏欧"。

六十二、浣溪沙·一曲新词酒一杯

北宋：晏殊

一曲新词酒一杯，
去年天气旧亭台。
夕阳西下几时回？

无可奈何花落去，
似曾相识燕归来。
小园香径独徘徊。

62. Tune to "The Yarn-washing Stream"·I Drink a Cup When Finishing a New Lyric

Northern Song Dynasty: Yan Shu

I drink a cup when finishing a new lyric;
The weather and the pavilion remain the same as last year.
When will the sun, after setting, come back?

Unwilling yet helpless, the flowers fall;
Swallows, seemingly acquainted, have returned to the hall.
Back and forth, I pace on the scented lane in the garden small.

作者简介

欧阳修（1007年—1072年），字永叔，号醉翁、六一居士；生于绵州（今四川绵阳），吉州永丰（今江西吉安永丰县）人，北宋政治家、文学家。吉州原属庐陵郡，故以"庐陵欧阳修"自居。官至参知政事（副宰相），谥号文忠，世称欧阳文忠公。

欧阳修与韩愈、柳宗元、苏轼合称"千古文章四大家"；与韩愈、柳宗元、苏洵、苏轼、苏辙、王安石、曾巩被后世称为"唐宋散文八大家"。

他四岁而孤，依于叔父而长；自幼敏悟过人，以荻画地学书。1030年，赐进士出身；据主考官晏殊说，因其锋芒毕露，欲促其成才，故挫其锐。

欧阳修仕途多舛，三遭贬谪。他主张除积弊、行宽简、与民休息；与范仲淹、韩琦、富弼等推行"庆历新政"，改革吏治、军事、贡举法等。新政失败，被贬为滁州（今安徽滁州）太守，写下不朽名篇《醉翁亭记》。

1057年，欧阳修主持进士考试，以其识人之明，录取苏洵、苏轼、苏辙、曾巩等人。此外，他举荐了王安石、韩琦、司马光、程颢、吕大钧、包拯等。"唐宋八大家"中，宋代其余五人均出其门下，堪称千古伯乐。

欧阳修师承韩愈，引领宋代诗文革新，主张明道致用。他一生写了五百余篇散文，无论叙事说理、抒情写景，均文风平易，内容翔实，深入浅出，洗练流畅，一改前朝浮靡文风。

欧阳修撰写了史上第一部牡丹培植学术专著《洛阳牡丹记》。

哈佛大学著名汉学家宇文所安认为：欧阳修的渊博和睿智，可与英语文学中的塞缪尔·约翰逊相提并论。

六十三、蝶恋花·庭院深深深几许

北宋：欧阳修

庭院深深深几许，
杨柳堆烟，
帘幕无重数。
玉勒雕鞍游冶处，
楼高不见章台路。

雨横风狂三月暮，
门掩黄昏，
无计留春住。
泪眼问花花不语，
乱红飞过秋千去。

63. Tune to "Butterflies' Love of Flowers"·The Courtyard Is Deep, Yet, How Deep Is It?

Northern Song Dynasty: Ouyang Xiu

The courtyard is deep, yet, how deep is it?
From weeping willows rise layers of mist;
Curtains, one behind another, are countless.
Jade bits and gorgeous saddles are around brothels;
Climbing high towers, she sees no Zhangtai Street for courtesans.

At the end of the third lunar month, rain is pouring and wind is wild;
Doors have been closed to keep dusk inside;
She can find no way to keep spring.
Tears in eyes, she asked the flowers and they said nothing;
Scattering fallen flowers are fluttering past the swing.

作者简介

王安石（1021年—1086年），字介甫，号半山，临川（今江西抚州临川区）人，北宋思想家、政治家、文学家、改革家。1079年，被封为"荆国公"，世称王荆公；1086年，病逝于钟山（今江苏南京）；1094年，谥"文"，后世称王文公。

王安石出身官宦世家；1042年，登进士榜第四名，任职地方，体恤民情，扩办学校，治绩斐然；1058年，上万言书，批判官制、科举弊端，揭露政府奢靡之风，提出"收天下之财以供天下之费"，请求改革政治。

1070年，王安石拜为宰相，改革财政、军事、科举制度，以期扭转北宋积贫积弱局势。其变法使得"国富兵强"，但"民贫"，可见其法"聚敛民财"、"以国为本"；王安石急于求成，重用投机分子，导致"新旧党争"，削弱了北宋统治。

王安石推动诗文革新，主张文道合一，提倡朴实文风，强调"文以致用"。其前期诗歌关注社会，反映民间疾苦，重说理，轻韵味；后期以景物诗为主，重意炼辞，含蓄深沉，丰神远韵，自成一家，世称"王荆公体"。其散文揭露时弊，政治色彩浓厚；论说文观点鲜明，分析深刻，语言精练，逻辑、概括性强；其短文简洁峻切，有"瘦硬通神"的独特风格；其词空阔苍茫、淡远纯朴，与范仲淹共开豪放词之先声。

梁启超曾称王安石："三代下求完人，惟公庶足以当之矣。"

六十四、梅花

北宋：王安石

墙角数枝梅，
凌寒独自开。
遥知不是雪，
为有暗香来。

64. Plum Blossom

Northern Song Dynasty: Wang Anshi

On the wall's corner are several branches of Chinese plum;

Facing the biting cold, they risk their lives to blossom.

From afar, I know it is not snow,

Since through the air, secret fragrance is coming to me.

作者简介

苏轼（1037年—1101年），字子瞻，号东坡居士，世称苏东坡、苏仙，眉州眉山（今四川眉山市）人，北宋文学家、书法家、画家、美食家。

苏轼开创了"豪放"词派，与辛弃疾并称"苏辛"；其诗题材广阔，豪健清新，与黄庭坚并称"苏黄"；其散文豪放自如，纵横恣肆，与欧阳修并称"欧苏"，为"唐宋八大家"之一。

1057年，苏轼、苏辙兄弟同榜进士及第。1071年，苏轼上书论王安石变法弊端。1079年，因"乌台诗案"，苏轼险遭杀身之祸；王安石上书："安有圣世而杀才士乎？"（宋太祖赵匡胤曾定下不杀士大夫之国策），苏轼得以逃过一劫。

1085年，司马光拜相，尽废新法；苏轼谏议、抨击旧党腐败。苏轼既不容于新党，又不见谅于旧党。1097年，苏轼被放逐儋州（今海南儋州）；学人至儋州，从苏轼学。1101年，苏轼逝世；后追赠为太师，谥号"文忠"。

苏轼认为诗、词同源，提出词应"自是一家"。他突破音乐对词体的束缚，开拓了词境，使词成为独立诗体。苏轼诗歌表现力惊人，万物皆可入诗；在题材、形式和情思方面，超越了同代诗人。苏轼散文挥洒如意，气势雄放，语言平易；他推崇韩、欧古文，认为文章应具有艺术价值，而不仅是"文以载道"。

其书法自成一家，与黄庭坚、米芾、蔡襄并称"宋四家"。其画重神似，主张画外有情，反对形似，提倡"诗画本一津，天工与清新"，并提出"士人画"的概念，对后代"文人画"的发展奠定了理论基础。其美学思想亦成为范式：万物皆有可观。

苏轼重视人才培养，黄庭坚、张耒、晁补之、秦观合称"苏门四学士"；加上陈师道和李廌，又合称"苏门六君子"。此外，李格非、李之仪、唐庚等深受苏轼影响。

苏轼的人生态度为后代文人所景仰：进退自如，宠辱不惊，坚持操守，全生养性。研究者认为，苏轼"宁为民碎、不为官全"，其"民本思想"和"富民"主张具有划时代的历史意义。

王国维评价苏轼："若无文学之天才，其人格亦自足千古。"2000年，法国《世界报》把苏轼誉为"一千年来影响世界进程的千年英雄"。

六十五、水调歌头·明月几时有

北宋：苏轼

丙辰中秋，欢饮达旦，大醉。作此篇，兼怀子由。

明月几时有？
把酒问青天。
不知天上宫阙，
今夕是何年。
我欲乘风归去，
又恐琼楼玉宇，
高处不胜寒。
起舞弄清影，
何似在人间？

转朱阁，
低绮户，
照无眠。
不应有恨，
何事长向别时圆？
人有悲欢离合，
月有阴晴圆缺，
此事古难全。
但愿人长久，
千里共婵娟。

65. Tune to "Overture to Song of Water"·When Did the Bright Moon First Appear?

Northern Song Dynasty: Su Shi

On the Mid-Autumn Day of 1076, I drank happily till the next morning and got heavily drunk. I wrote this poem while missing my younger brother Ziyou.

When did the bright moon first appear?
Wine in hand, I ask the blue sky to make it clear.
In the celestial palaces, I am wondering,
What day it is tonight when I am drinking.
I want to go back on the wings of wind,
Yet the jade edifices on the moon, I am afraid,
May be too high and too cold for me.
Fairy Chang'e is dancing there lonely;
Would not it be better to live in the world?

The moon went around the vermilion-colored tower,
And hang low on the painted and carved windows of the chamber;
It shone brightly upon the sleepless heart.
Towards man, the moon cannot feel resentment, for my part;
Yet, why does it turn the fullest when people are apart?
Life is full of sorrow, joy, separation, and reunion;
Dim or bright, the moon waxes or wanes freely;
The world has never been as perfect as we want it to be.
May each of us be blessed with longevity!
Though thousands of miles apart, we can share the moon's beauty.

六十六、念奴娇·赤壁怀古

北宋：苏轼

大江东去，
浪淘尽，
千古风流人物。
故垒西边，
人道是，
三国周郎赤壁。
乱石穿空，
惊涛拍岸，
卷起千堆雪。
江山如画，
一时多少豪杰。

遥想公瑾当年，
小乔初嫁了，
雄姿英发，
羽扇纶巾。
谈笑间，
樯橹灰飞烟灭。
故国神游，
多情应笑我，
早生华发。
人生如梦，
一樽还酹江月。

66. Tune to "The Beautiful Niannu"·Meditation on the Distant Past on the Red Cliffs

Northern Song Dynasty: Su Shi

The Yangtze River runs eastward;
Its waves have outlived
All heroes and celebrities in human history.
To the west are ruins of camps of an ancient military army;
It is said that
It is the Red Cliffs where General Zhou of the Three Kingdoms fought.
Into the sky, cliffs stick up erect;
Against the banks thunderous waves beat;
Spindrift rolls up like a thousand piles of snow drifting.
The spectacular River and mountains resemble a painting
Within a short time, heroes surged like rain pouring.

I think far back to General Zhou's time;
The matchless beauty Little Qiao just married him.
He was a valiant and gallant young man,
A feather fan in his hand, his hair fastened with a cyan silk ribbon.
While he was talking and laughing,
His great enemy's warships were burned, ashes scattering.
I am daydreaming of visiting the Eastern Han Dynasty;
The tender and loving Little Qiao would laugh at me,
For at such an early age, grey-haired I have become.
Life is just like a dream;
Pouring wine, I pay homage to the moon on the great stream.

六十七、江城子·乙卯正月二十日夜记梦

北宋：苏轼

十年生死两茫茫，
不思量，
自难忘。
千里孤坟，
无处话凄凉。
纵使相逢应不识，
尘满面，
鬓如霜。

夜来幽梦忽还乡，
小轩窗，
正梳妆。
相顾无言，
惟有泪千行。
料得年年肠断处，
明月夜，
短松冈。

67. Tune to "Song of Nanjing"·To Record My Dream on the Night of the 20th of the First Month of the Lunar Year, 1075

Northern Song Dynasty: Su Shi

After you died, for ten years, we have been missing each other in vain.

I did not mean to miss you, but again and again,

I just cannot forget you, my love.

A thousand miles away is your lonely grave;

There is no place for me to tell you my forlornness.

You will not recognize me, even if we met face to face;

My face is coated in dust,

And my temples are as white as frost.

Last night, in a vague dream, I suddenly returned home;

In front of our little chamber window, with a comb,

You were brushing and detangling your hair.

We looked at each other, speechless, and there,

Only tears streamed down endlessly from our eyes.

I believe, every year, the place to shatter our hearts into pieces

Must be, on each moonlit night,

The hill where small pine trees are in sight.

六十八、临江仙·夜归临皋

北宋：苏轼

夜饮东坡醒复醉，
归来仿佛三更。
家童鼻息已雷鸣。
敲门都不应，
倚杖听江声。

长恨此身非我有，
何时忘却营营？
夜阑风静縠纹平。
小舟从此逝，
江海寄余生。

68. Tune to "Riverside Daffodils"·Returning to Lingao at Night

Northern Song: Su Shi

Drinking at night at the East Slope, I sobered up and got drunk again;
When I returned home, it was almost midnight then.
The boy servants were snoring thunderously.
I knocked at the door, yet no one answered me.
Leaning on my walking stick, I listened to the Yangtze.

Very often, I hate myself for not owning my own body;
When can I forget the hustle and bustle of life completely?
Night deepening, the wind was getting tranquil and smooth.
How I long to get myself a little boat and sail around the earth;
I just want to spend the rest of my life on the sea and the Yangtze.

六十九、卜算子·黄州定慧院寓居作

北宋：苏轼

缺月挂疏桐，
漏断人初静。
谁见幽人独往来，
缥缈孤鸿影。

惊起却回头，
有恨无人省。
拣尽寒枝不肯栖，
寂寞沙洲冷。

69. Tune to "Song of the Fortune-Teller"·A Poem Written at Dinghui Temple Where I Lodge

Northern Song Dynasty: Su Shi

Hanging from the sparse phoenix tree is the waning moon;
The clepsydra has stopped; people are starting to turn quiet.
Who can see the solitary man come and go alone?
I am a lone wild goose, faraway and lost.

I am flushed, and yet look back for no reason;
Feeling bitter in my heart, I am not understood.
Surveying all frozen twigs, I will not perch on one;
The lonely lake isle I prefer is cold.

作者简介

李之仪（约1048年—约1128年），字端叔，自号姑溪居士、姑溪老农。沧州无棣（今山东庆云县）人。

早年师从范仲淹之子范纯仁，1070年中进士，官至原州（今属甘肃）通判。宋哲宗元祐年末，成为苏轼门人；与黄庭坚、秦观等交往甚密，是"元祐"文人集团的重要成员。因与苏轼的关系，他仕途多舛；苏轼流放外地时，李之仪积极联系旧日好友和官宦，以图苏轼早返京师。

李之仪擅长作词，其词"多次韵"，小令更长于淡语、景语、情语（毛晋《姑溪词跋》）。受苏轼的熏陶，其文章"神锋俊逸，有苏轼之体"。

七十、卜算子·我住长江头

北宋：李之仪

我住长江头，
君住长江尾。
日日思君不见君，
共饮长江水。
此水几时休，
此恨何时已。
只愿君心似我心，
定不负相思意。

70. Tune to "Song of the Fortune-Teller"·I Live Upstream of the Yangtze River

Northern Song Dynasty: Li Zhiyi

I live upstream of the Yangtze River;

You live downstream of the Yangtze River.

Day in, day out, I miss you, and yet see no you;

We drink together water of the Yangtze.

When will the river dry up?

When will the parting sorrow stop?

If only your heart was like my heart!

I will never be unworthy of your love, sweetheart.

作者简介

岳飞（1103年—1142年），字鹏举，相州汤阴县永和乡孝悌里（今河南安阳汤阴县程岗村）人，中国历史上著名军事家、战略家，民族英雄，位列南宋"中兴四将"之首。

岳飞少读兵书、习武，1122年，离家从戎。1127年四月，北宋灭亡；岳飞耻于"靖康之耻"，上书宋高宗，劝其率军北渡，光复中原，得"小臣越职，非所宜言"批语，被革除军职、军籍。

岳飞"精忠报国"，四次从戎，率岳家军征战十一年，所向披靡。1140年，完颜兀术毁盟攻宋；岳飞挥师北伐，收复失地。宋高宗、秦桧以十二道"金字牌"诏回岳飞，1142年一月，以"莫须有"罪名杀害了他。

宋孝宗时，岳飞冤狱被平反，改葬于西湖畔栖霞岭；追谥武穆，后又追谥忠武，封鄂王。

岳飞诗词慷慨激昂，气势磅礴，结构严谨；其书法以行、草为主，畅快淋漓，气韵生动，意态精密。

孙中山曾言："岳飞魂，是中华民族的精神代表，也就是民族魂。"

七十一、满江红·写怀

南宋：岳飞

怒发冲冠，
凭栏处，
潇潇雨歇。
抬望眼，
仰天长啸，
壮怀激烈。
三十功名尘与土，
八千里路云和月。
莫等闲，
白了少年头，
空悲切。

靖康耻，
犹未雪。
臣子恨，
何时灭？
驾长车，
踏破贺兰山缺。
壮志饥餐胡虏肉，
笑谈渴饮匈奴血。
待从头
收拾旧山河，
朝天阙。

71. Tune to "Red Water Fern"·To Express Emotions

Southern Song Dynasty: Yue Fei

My furious hair thrusts against my hat;

I am leaning against the railing;

The drizzle has just stopped.

My eyes I am raising;

Looking up to the sky, I let out a long and loud cry;

In my heart, aspirations are boiling.

My thirty years' accomplishments are nothing but dust dry;

In the eight-thousand-mile fighting, the moon shone, clouds floating.

Idle not your time away,

Or when your hair turns gray,

You can only repent in vain all day.

The Humiliation of the Jingkang Period[①]

Has not yet been wiped out.

A subject's hatred!

When will it melt?

A war chariot I will drive determinedly

To tread on the Helan Mountains' valley.

Bravely, I will eat northern barbarians' flesh when hungry;

Laughing and talking, I will drink my enemies' blood when thirsty.

I will start all over again, and

Resolve to recover the lost land,

And report the good news to Heaven firsthand.

---

① **The Humiliation of Jingkang Period:** also called the Jingkang Incident. It took place in 1127 when invading Jurchen soldiers from the Jin Dynasty besieged and sacked Bianjing (Kaifeng), the capital of the Song Dynasty of China. The Jin forces abducted Emperor Qinzong, his father Emperor Emeritus Huizong, along with many members of the imperial court. This ended the era known as the Northern Song Dynasty, when the Song Dynasty controlled most of China. The rest of the imperial family was forced to flee and establish a new government, now known as the Southern Song. This incident is so named because this was the major incident during the short reign of Emperor Qinzong, whose era name was "Jingkang."

作者简介

李清照（1084 年—1155 年），号易安居士，齐州章丘（今山东章丘）人；婉约词派代表人物，有"千古第一才女"之称。

其父李格非藏书甚富，精通经史，长于散文。在其父熏陶下，李清照自小文采过人。十八岁，李清照与金石家赵明诚结婚；北宋灭亡，与夫南渡，生活困顿；1129 年，赵明诚卒于建康（今南京）。1131 年三月，李清照赴越（今浙江绍兴），书画被盗，金石古卷散佚，饱受打击。

南渡前生活优裕，其词多闺阁之怨、离行之思；晚景孤苦凄凉，诗作多慨叹身世，凄怆沉郁，充满对国破家亡的忧思。

李清照善于白描，其词通俗淡雅，朴素自然，不见凿痕，达到完美之境界；从音乐维度讲，其词音韵和谐，旋津柔美，情感细腻，节奏幽怨涂缓。

李清照在词坛独树一帜，形成了独特的"易安体"。

七十二、声声慢·寻寻觅觅

南宋：李清照

寻寻觅觅，
冷冷清清，
凄凄惨惨戚戚。
乍暖还寒时候，
最难将息。
三杯两盏淡酒，
怎敌他、晚来风急？
雁过也，
正伤心，
却是旧时相识。

满地黄花堆积。
憔悴损，
如今有谁堪摘？
守着窗儿，
独自怎生得黑？
梧桐更兼细雨，
到黄昏、点点滴滴。
这次第，
怎一个愁字了得！

72. Tune to "A Note-by-note Slow Song"·Seek Seek, Prowl Prowl

Southern Song Dynasty: Li Qingzhao

Seek seek, prowl prowl;

Desolate desolate, cheerless cheerless;

Miserable miserable, tragic tragic, sorrowful sorrowful.

The sun warm, the wind chilly, the fickle weather is heartless;

To take good care of one's health now is the hardest thing.

How can two or three cups of wine drink

Avail against a sudden gust of wind in the evening?

Wild geese are flying across the sky before I can blink,

While I am just feeling broken-hearted;

Unexpectedly, the wild geese and I are already acquainted.

Heaps of yellow chrysanthemum flowers fill the flowerbed.

I am dreadfully pining away;

Who would come to pick them instead?

By the window I stay;

How can I make it through the day alone?

A drizzle is falling upon the phoenix trees;

When dusk descends, it is still drizzling in a sad tone.

Such scenes

Are regrettably beyond the word "Sorrow"!

七十三、如梦令·常记溪亭日暮

南宋：李清照

常记溪亭日暮，
沉醉不知归路。
兴尽晚回舟，
误入藕花深处。
争渡，争渡，
惊起一滩鸥鹭。

73. Tune to "A Dreamlike Short Lyric"·I Often Recall the Evening in a Waterside Pavilion

Southern Song Dynasty: Li Qingzhao

I often recall the evening in a waterside pavilion;
Highly intoxicated, I could not find my way home.
It being late, I rowed a boat back after all the fun;
Getting lost, I was deep into the lotus flowers.
I rowed harder and harder;
Gulls and egrets were startled and flew.

七十四、如梦令·昨夜雨疏风骤

南宋：李清照

昨夜雨疏风骤，
浓睡不消残酒。
试问卷帘人，
却道海棠依旧。
知否，知否？
应是绿肥红瘦。

74. Tune to "A Dreamlike Short Lyric"·Last Night, the Rain Was Light, the Wind Sudden

Southern Song Dynasty: Li Qingzhao

Last night, the rain was light, the wind sudden;
A sound sleep could not rid the hangover.
Timidly, I inquired of the maid pulling the bead curtain,
And she said Chinese crabapple flowers were blooming as ever.
Do you know? Do you know?
It should be the time when leaves are lush and flowers blow.

作者简介

辛弃疾（1140年—1207年），字幼安，号稼轩，济南府历城县（今济南历城区）人。南宋豪放派词人、将领，有"词中之龙"之称；与苏轼合称"苏辛"。

辛弃疾生于金国，以报国雪耻为志。1161年，辛弃疾参加耿京起义军；1162年，他奉命南下与朝廷联络，耿京被叛徒杀害，辛弃疾遂率五十多人袭击几万人的敌营，擒叛徒，归南宋。

辛弃疾痛恨腐败，于百姓宽厚，于下属官吏严苛。他认为，真正该严格管理的是官吏，而不是平民百姓。辛弃疾在官场备受排挤，虽政绩斐然，但深感壮志难酬，故屡次辞免。

1207年十月，辛弃疾愤然离世，临终大呼"杀贼！杀贼！"（《康熙济南府志·人物志》）。1275年，追赠为少师，谥号"忠敏"。

辛弃疾延续了苏轼之词豪放阔大、高旷开朗的风格，且以蔑视陈规的气概、过人的学养和才华，开拓了词更为广阔的天地。辛弃疾笔下景物多有一种奔腾耸峙的气概，故苏词潇洒疏朗、旷达超迈，而辛词则慷慨悲歌、激情飞扬。

苏轼以诗为词，而辛弃疾则以文为词。辛词的语言更加自由奔放，变化无端，广泛地引用经、史、子典籍和前人之诗。

《四库全书总目提要》说："其词慷慨纵横，有不可一世之概，于倚声家为变调，而异军突起，能于剪红刻翠之外，屹然别立一宗。"

七十五、永遇乐·京口北固亭怀古

南宋：辛弃疾

千古江山，
英雄无觅孙仲谋处。
舞榭歌台，
风流总被雨打风吹去。
斜阳草树，
寻常巷陌，
人道寄奴曾住。
想当年，
金戈铁马，
气吞万里如虎。

元嘉草草，
封狼居胥，
赢得仓皇北顾。
四十三年，
望中犹记，
烽火扬州路。
可堪回首，
佛狸祠下，
一片神鸦社鼓。
凭谁问：
廉颇老矣，
尚能饭否？

75. Tune to "Receiving Happy News Forever"·Meditation on the Distant Past at Beigu Pavilion in Jingkou

Southern Song Dynasty: Xin Qiji

Rivers and mountains, age-old, are still there and serene;
The hero Sun Quan, Emperor Da of Wu, is nowhere to be seen.
The dance performance pavilion and the singing stage, in vain,
With the hero, have always been washed away by wind and rain.
The setting sun shines upon grass and trees in a lane,
Which is just so ordinary and plain,
And where, as is said, Emperor Wu of Liu Song lived in childhood.
Think back to the years of his manhood,
Holding golden halberds and riding armored horses,
His army, like roaring tigers, rushed into the enemies.

Emperor Wen of Liu Song was rash and hasty;
He wanted to worship heaven in Langjuxu Mountain with a victory,
Yet he ended up in defeat and fled south, looking back in fear.
For forty-three years, I have been back south, by the end of the year;
Looking at the Central Plain, I still remember
Along the roads of Yangzhou, killings and burnings by the Jin soldiers;
How can I bear to look back at the evil!
At the foot of Emperor Taiwu of Northern Wei Memorial Temple,
Crows are pecking sacrifices and villagers are playing drums.
Who would ask the question anywhere but in poems?
"General Lianpo is old now;
Can he still eat like a horse anyhow?"

七十六、青玉案·元夕

南宋：辛弃疾

东风夜放花千树，
更吹落，
星如雨。
宝马雕车香满路。
凤箫声动，
玉壶光转，
一夜鱼龙舞。

蛾儿雪柳黄金缕，
笑语盈盈暗香去。
众里寻他千百度，
蓦然回首，
那人却在，
灯火阑珊处。

76. Tune to "Green Jade Tray"·The Lantern Festival

Southern Song Dynasty: Xin Qiji

Like a thousand trees blooming on a spring night, fireworks are set off,

And then in the wind, the flowers blow off

As if they are showers of twinkling stars.

In the street are fine steeds, perfume and luxury carriages;

The music of pan flutes[①] floats around;

The bright moon is heading westbound;

For the whole night, fish and loong lanterns dance around.

Women, silk moths and fontanesia and gold threads on their heads,

Smile and chat, and behind them, the secret fragrance spreads.

A thousand times, I looked for her in the crowd;

Suddenly, I turned around,

And she was right there,

The place where lanterns were rare.

---

① **pan flute:** also known as panpipe or syrinx. It is a musical instrument based on the principle of the closed tube, consisting of multiple pipes of gradually increasing length (and occasionally girth). Multiple varieties of pan flutes have been popular as folk instruments. The pipes are typically made from bamboo, giant cane, or local reeds. Other materials include wood, plastic, metal and ivory.

七十七、菩萨蛮·书江西造口壁

南宋：辛弃疾

郁孤台下清江水，
中间多少行人泪！
西北望长安，
可怜无数山。

青山遮不住，
毕竟东流去。
江晚正愁余，
山深闻鹧鸪。

77. Tune to "The Southern Buddha"·An Inscription on a Wall in Zaokou of Jiangxi

Southern Song Dynasty: Xin Qiji

At the foot of the Lushly Solitary Tower flows a clear river of water;
In it, countless tears are from civilians fleeing the war disaster!
I look northwest towards Chang'an eagerly;
Sadly, I see numerous mountains only.

Green mountains cannot block my longing;
After all, the river keeps flowing to the east.
The sun setting above the river, I feel disconsolate;
At this time, deep in the hill, I hear partridges chirping.

七十八、丑奴儿·书博山道中壁

南宋：辛弃疾

少年不识愁滋味，
爱上层楼。
爱上层楼，
为赋新词强说愁。

而今识尽愁滋味，
欲说还休。
欲说还休。
却道天凉好个秋。

78. Tune to "The Ugly Kid"·A Lyric Written on the Rock Face of Boshan Hill

Southern Song Dynasty: Xin Qiji

As a youth, I knew not what sorrow was;
I loved to climb up high towers.
I loved to climb up high towers;
To write a new lyric, I pretended to have sorrows.

Now, I have tasted all sorrows;
Wanting to talk about them, I keep my mouth closed.
Wanting to talk about them, I keep my mouth closed;
Yet, what I say is: how cool the good autumn is.

作者简介

陆游（1125年—1210年），字务观，号放翁，越州山阴（今浙江绍兴）人，南宋文学家、史学家、爱国诗人。

陆游生于江南名门望族，"靖康之耻"对其影响至深，一生以收复国土为己任。1154年，陆游参加礼部考试，因秦桧嫉恨，未被录取。1158年，秦桧病逝，陆游初入仕途；任职多地，因坚持抗金，遭主和派排斥，陆游屡次辞免。1210年，陆游壮志难酬，与世长辞，留绝笔诗《示儿》。

陆游工于诗、词、文，自言"六十年间万首诗"。前期诗作重文字形式；中期之作宏肆奔放；晚期之诗清旷淡远。其诗语言平易晓畅、章法谨严，兼具李白之雄奇浪漫与杜甫之沉郁现实；其诗爱国主义情感影响深远。其词风格多变，兼有苏轼之豪放和晏殊之婉约；其散文构思奇巧，文笔精纯。

赵翼曾言：宋诗以苏、陆为两大家，后人震于东坡之名，注注谓苏胜于陆，而不知陆实胜苏也。（陆游之诗）少工藻绘，中务宏肆，晚造平淡。朝廷之上，无不以划疆守盟、息事宁人为上策，而放翁独以复仇雪耻，长篇短咏，寓其悲愤。

七十九、卜算子·咏梅

南宋：陆游

驿外断桥边，
寂寞开无主。
已是黄昏独自愁，
更著风和雨。
无意苦争春，
一任群芳妒。
零落成泥碾作尘，
只有香如故。

79. Tune to "Song of the Fortune-Teller"·On Chinese Plum

Southern Song Dynasty: Lu You

Outside the courier station, beside the broken bridge,
A wild Chinese plum is blossoming without foliage.
Dusk around and alone, plum blossoms feel sorrowful,
While wind blasts and heavy showers make them tremble.
They have not the least desire to be the herald of spring,
Thus caring nothing about other flowers' envying.
The blossoms scatter and are crushed into mud and dust;
Nothing is left but the same fragrance pervading the wind gust.

八十、钗头凤·红酥手

南宋：陆游

红酥手，
黄縢酒，
满城春色宫墙柳。
东风恶，
欢情薄。
一怀愁绪，
几年离索。
错、错、错！

春如旧，
人空瘦，
泪痕红浥鲛绡透。
桃花落，
闲池阁。
山盟虽在，
锦书难托。
莫、莫、莫！

80. Tune to "A Phoenix Hairpin"·Rosy, Soft Hands

Southern Song Dynasty: Lu You

Your rosy, soft hands shine;

A yellow-silk-sealed bottle of wine,

Spring is all over the city, willows weaving in the palace.

The east wind is fierce;

So short was our happy time.

In my bosom, sorrows chime;

In these years of separation, I have been lonely all along.

Wrong, wrong, wrong!

Spring is the same as ever;

Yearning in vain, you have become thinner and thinner;

Tears have washed off your rouge, your silk handkerchief soaking.

Peach flowers are falling;

Over the pond, the pavilion is empty.

Vows to love forever, though, are still as sweet as honey,

Letters written on silk cloth cannot be sent to you.

Let go, let go, let go!

作者简介

唐婉（1128年—1156年），字蕙仙，浙江绍兴人。

据《赠亡妻》，唐婉乃郑州通判唐闳的独生女儿，母亲李氏媛，祖父是北宋末年鸿儒少卿唐翊。唐婉自幼文静灵秀、才华横溢；陆家以一只精美无比的家传凤钗作信物，与唐家订亲。

陆游与唐婉成婚，鸾凤和鸣；陆母不满，认为唐婉耽误陆游前程，命陆游休妻。陆游另筑别院，安置唐婉，其母察觉，命陆游另娶。

数年后，陆游游沈园，偶遇唐婉夫妇。唐婉征得丈夫赵士程同意，亲手向陆游敬了一杯酒。陆游饮后，在沈园题写了《钗头凤》一词，遂搁笔而去。唐婉返家，难抑悲恸，和了一曲，不久抑郁而终。

八十一、钗头凤·世情薄

南宋：唐婉

世情薄，
人情恶，
雨送黄昏花易落。
晓风干，
泪痕残。
欲笺心事，
独语斜阑。
难，难，难！

人成各，
今非昨，
病魂常似秋千索。
角声寒，
夜阑珊。
怕人寻问，
咽泪装欢。
瞒，瞒，瞒！

81. Tune to "A Phoenix Hairpin"·The World Is Cold

Southern Song Dynasty: Tang Wan

The world is cold;

Human hearts are malicious;

Rain pouring at dusk, down to the earth peach flowers rolled.

At dawn, the breeze dried my face;

On my cheeks, there are tear stains.

Wanting to write down my inner feelings,

I murmured alone, leaning on the slanting railing in the yard.

Hard, hard, hard !

We have been separated;

The good old days cannot be re-found.

Illness is like a swing and I have been haunted.

I felt chilly with the painted bugle's sound;

The night is coming to an end.

Afraid I may be asked about what has happened,

I swallowed my tears and pretended to smile.

Beguile, beguile, beguile!

作者简介

赵师秀（1170年—1219年），字紫芝，号灵秀，亦称灵芝，又号天乐。永嘉（今浙江温州）人。宋太祖八世孙，南宋诗人；与徐照、徐玑、翁卷并称"永嘉四灵"，人称"鬼才"，开创了"江湖派"诗风。

1190年，赵师秀中进士；1195年，任上元主簿，后为筠州（今江西高安）推官。仕途不佳，晚年宦游，寓居钱塘，逝于临安，葬于西湖。

赵师秀善五律，尚白描，苦心雕琢，锤炼字句，以表现凄清心境和淡泊情怀。他编选了《二妙集》和《众妙集》两集，以晚唐诗法为宗，诗学"姚贾（姚合、贾岛）"，影响了大量江湖诗人，打破了生硬晦涩的江西诗派独霸南宋末诗坛的局面。

《约客》融诗、画为一体，情景交融，清新隽永，和谐精妙，回味无穷。

八十二、约客

南宋：赵师秀

黄梅时节家家雨，
青草池塘处处蛙。
有约不来过夜半，
闲敲棋子落灯花。

82. Waiting for a Guest

Southern Song Dynasty: Zhao Shixiu

When plums are yellow, rain comes to each family;
All over the grass of ponds, frogs can be heard noisily.
The expected guest has not come even after midnight;
I idly tap the table with a Go stone, snuff off the candlelight.

作者简介

文天祥(1236年—1283年),字宋瑞,又字履善;道号文山。江西吉州庐陵(今江西吉安)人,南宋政治家、爱国诗人、民族英雄,与陆秀夫、张世杰并称"宋末三杰"。

1256年,文天祥状元及第,一心为国,官至右丞相兼枢密使。南宋投降,文天祥坚持抗元,直至被俘。1279年,宋、元崖山决战,南宋覆灭。忽必烈劝降文天祥,许于高官;文天祥坚贞不屈,三年后,慷慨就义。

文天祥前期之诗清新、豪放、斗志昂扬;后期之作悲壮、沉痛、典雅,多感叹人生险阻艰难。

毛泽东评:"命系庖厨何足惜哉",此言不当。岳飞、文天祥、戴名世、瞿秋白……以身殉志,不亦伟乎。蒋介石言:(文天祥)代表整个中华民族之精神与人格,并为整个民族万古不变的光荣。

八十三、过零丁洋

南宋:文天祥

辛苦遭逢起一经,
干戈寥落四周星。
山河破碎风飘絮,
身世浮沉雨打萍。
惶恐滩头说惶恐,
零丁洋里叹零丁。
人生自古谁无死,
留取丹心照汗青。

83. To Pass the Lonely Sea

Southern Song Dynasty: Wen Tianxiang

All my hardships and sufferings start from my learning;

Only a scattering of skirmishes is around after four years' fighting.

Like willow catkins in the wind, the country is too broken to maintain;

Life's ups and downs have made me like duckweeds in heavy rain.

Before the Fearful River Beach, I talked about fear;

In the Lonely Sea, I sighed for loneliness.

Who can but die in this world dear?

I will leave my loyal heart forever in the annals.

作者简介

蒋捷（约1245年—1305年后），字胜欲，号竹山，南宋词人，宋末元初阳羡（今江苏宜兴）人；人称"竹山先生""樱桃进士"。

蒋捷出身宜兴大族；1274年中进士。南宋覆灭，怀亡国之痛，隐居不仕，其气节为时人所重。

蒋捷善于词，与周密、王沂孙、张炎并称"宋末四大家"。蒋捷之词情调凄清、悲凉疏爽，哀亡国之痛，抒不屈之民族气节；其词风格多样，兼具豪放派的清奇流畅与婉约派的含蓄蕴藉，独具一格，对清初阳羡派词人影响颇深。

清代文学评论家刘熙载说："蒋竹山词未极流动自然，然洗练缜密，语多创获。"

八十四、虞美人·听雨

南宋：蒋捷

少年听雨歌楼上，
红烛昏罗帐。
壮年听雨客舟中，
江阔云低断雁叫西风。
而今听雨僧庐下，
鬓已星星也。
悲欢离合总无情，
一任阶前点滴到天明。

84. Tune to "Beauty Yu"·Listening to the Rain

Southern Song Dynasty: Jiang Jie

In my twenties, I listened to the rain in a courtesan's upstairs chamber;
In the red candle light, the canopy bed curtains were even dimmer.
In my forties, I listened to the rain in a traveler boat,
Wide rivers, low clouds, the west wind, a lost wild goose's cry afloat.
Now, I listen to the rain in monks' dwellings;
My temples are as white as glistening stars.
Each is ruthless, sorrow or joy, separation or union;
Just let the droplets of drizzle fall before the stairs till dawn.

作者简介

关汉卿（1219年—1301年），晚号已斋、已斋叟；解州人（今山西运城），其籍贯有大都（今北京）人；祁州（今河北安国市）人等说；元代杂剧奠基人、戏剧作家；与白朴、马致远、郑光祖并称"元曲四大家"；被誉为"曲圣"。

元代熊梦祥《析津志辑佚·名宦》曰："关一斋，字汉卿，燕人。生而倜傥，博学能文。滑稽多智，蕴藉风流，为一时之冠……"

关汉卿的悲剧《窦娥冤》是中国古典悲剧典范，一百多年前，已被介绍到欧洲，"列之于世界大悲剧中亦无愧色"（王国维《宋元戏曲史》）；其喜剧风趣、幽默，是后代喜剧楷模；其杂剧在艺术构思、戏剧冲突、人物塑造、语言运用等方面，为后世所推崇。

世界和平理事会把关汉卿列为1958年纪念的"世界文化名人"。

八十五、四块玉·别情

元代：关汉卿

自送别，
心难舍，
一点相思几时绝？
凭阑袖拂杨花雪。
溪又斜，
山又遮，
人去也！

85. Tune to "Four Jades"·The Pain of Parting

Yuan Dynasty: Guan Hanqing

Since the day I saw you off,
In my heart, I could hardly tear myself away from you;
When will the traces of lovesickness die off?
I lean against the railing, using my sleeve to flick willow catkins off.
The stream is meandering;
My view the mountains are blocking;
So far away are you!

作者简介

白朴（1226年—约1306年），原名恒，字仁甫，后改名朴，字太素，号兰谷。汴梁（今河南开封）人，晚年寓居金陵（今江苏南京），终身未仕。元代著名杂剧作家，与关汉卿、马致远、郑光祖并称"元曲四大家"。

白朴出身士大夫家庭，少时历经战乱，母子相失，为瘟疫所袭，生命垂危，得元好问（金末至大蒙古国时期文学家、历史学家）救助。元好问对其悉心培养，但白朴厌恶蒙古统治者的残暴行径，放弃功名争逐，潜心词赋。

白朴善词曲，其词"词语道严，情寄高远"，承袭了元好问长短句的格调，跌宕沉详，天然古朴，多凄楚之调。其散曲多以本色语言抒写闲情逸致。

他善于利用历史题材，敷演故事，创造新意，且词采优美，情意绵长。据《录鬼簿》名目，白朴所作杂剧15种；现仅存《梧桐雨》和《墙头马上》；《梧桐雨》被列为元杂剧四大悲剧之一。

王国维曾说，《汉宫秋》"雄劲"，《梧桐雨》"悲壮"，可并称"千古绝品"。

八十六、天净沙·秋

元代：白朴

孤村落日残霞，
轻烟老树寒鸦，
一点飞鸿影下。
青山绿水，
白草红叶黄花。

86. Tune to "A Sandless Sky"·Autumn

Yuan Dynasty: Bai Pu

A lonely village, the setting sun, thin rosy clouds,
Soft smoke, old trees, jackdaws,
The tiny shadow of a wild goose is flying downwards.
Blue hills, green water,
White grass, red leaves, yellow flowers.

作者简介

马致远（约1251年—约1321年至1324年间），字千里，晚号东篱，大都（今北京）人，原籍河北东光县马祠堂村，著名戏曲家、杂剧家，被后人誉为"马神仙""曲状元"，"元曲四大家"之一。

马致远仕途坎坷；晚年辞官归隐，以衔杯击缶自娱。

在元代曲坛，马致远承前启后，以"叹世、超世"之表象，行"愤世、抗世"之深意。其散曲意境高远、音韵优美、语言疏宕、数量最多、流传最广；其杂剧脱离市井，多表现文人内心矛盾和苦闷，语言典丽精致，富有表现力；其小令《天净沙·秋思》匠心独运，自然天成，不见雕琢，被誉为"秋思之祖"。

八十七、天净沙·秋思

元代：马致远

枯藤老树昏鸦，
小桥流水人家。
古道西风瘦马。
夕阳西下，
断肠人在天涯。

87. Tune to "A Sandless Sky"·Autumn Thought

Yuan Dynasty: Ma Zhiyuan

Rotten rattan, an old tree, a dusk-time crow,
A small bridge, flowing water, a house,
An ancient path, the chilly west wind, a skinny horse.
The sun is setting and casting a reddish glow.
A shattered heart is in the distant place.

八十八、折桂令·春情

元代：徐再思

平生不会相思，
才会相思，
便害相思。
身似浮云，
心如飞絮，
气若游丝，
空一缕余香在此，
盼千金游子何之。
证候来时，
正是何时？
灯半昏时，
月半明时。

作者简介

徐再思（约1280年—1330年），字德可，号甜斋（或"甜齐"），浙江嘉兴人，元代散曲作家；曾任嘉兴路吏；因好食甘饴，故号甜斋。与自号酸斋的贯云石齐名，二人散曲合为一编，世称《酸甜乐府》。

徐再思工于散曲，善用俗谣俚曲；主题多为闺情春思、恋情、江南景物、归隐悠闲。其散曲清丽工巧，深沉娟秀，擅用白描，对仗工整。

88. Tune to "A Lyric of Picking Sweet Osmanthus Twigs"·Longing for Love

Yuan Dynasty: Xu Zaisi

Up to now, I am unable to feel lovesick;

I am just beginning to be able to feel lovesick,

And I am suffering from being lovesick.

My body is like floating clouds;

My heart resembles flying catkins;

My breath is the same as drifting spider silk.

There remains in vain a little wisp of his fragrance;

I am dying for my wandering sweetheart's lodging place.

When the symptoms of lovesickness come,

What is the exact time?

It is when the candle light is half dim;

It is when the moonlight is half bright.

作者简介

张可久（约1270年—约1350年），字小山（《录鬼簿》）；浙江庆元路（今浙江宁波鄞州区）人，元朝散曲家、剧作家、散曲"清丽派"代表作家；与乔吉并称"双璧"，与张养浩合称"二张"。现存小令800余首，为传世散曲最多的元代作家。

张可久怀才不遇，时官时隐，徜徉山水。其作品多记游怀古、赠答唱和、吟男女情思。他擅长写景状物，炼字断句，讲究格律音韵；其作品清丽典雅、对仗工整、字句和美。

张可久使元曲从"市井文学"转变为"文人文学"，其散曲被后世视为典范。明代朱权《太和正音谱》誉之为"词林之宗匠"。

八十九、殿前欢·离思

元代：张可久

月笼沙，
十年心事付琵琶。
相思懒看帏屏画，
人在天涯。
春残豆蔻花，
情寄鸳鸯帕，
香冷荼蘼架。
旧游台榭，
晓梦窗纱。

89. Tune to "Happiness at the Royal Court"·Thought on Parting

Yuan Dynasty: Zhang Kejiu

The moonlight is cloaking the sand;

Playing the pipa, I pour out my ten-year inner feelings.

Lovesick, I have no desire to look at the room divider's paintings;

My loved one is in the distant land.

In late spring, round cardamom is blossoming;

On a silk scarf a pair of mandarin ducks I am embroidering;

On the trellis, thimbleberry flowers are alone in bloom.

In my dream, I revisited the waterside pavilion;

Awaking at dawn, I gazed at the window's paper screen.

九十、题龙阳县青草湖

元代：唐珙

西风吹老洞庭波，
一夜湘君白发多。
醉后不知天在水，
满船清梦压星河。

作者简介

唐珙（生卒年不详），字温如，元末明初诗人；会稽山阴（今浙江绍兴）人。《全唐诗》误其为晚唐人；生平仅略见于《御选元诗》卷首《姓名爵里》和《元诗选补遗》小传。《大雅集》《元诗体要》《御选元诗》等选录其诗数首，清钱熙彦《元诗选补遗》编录其诗八首。

唐珙生平无记载，仅知"珙豪于诗"。其父唐珏是南宋词人、义士，曾于元僧盗掘南宋皇陵之时，出资请人偷拾诸帝遗骨，重新择地安葬，使遗骨免受元僧亵渎。

《题龙阳县青草湖》一诗充满浪漫主义色彩，前两句以虚写实，后两句以实写虚，诗境缥缈，构思独特，想象奇丽，笔调轻灵，颇具唐诗品格。诗人写景叙梦，虚实一体，奇幻浪漫，超凡脱俗，实乃古今关于洞庭湖的第一诗。

90. On Green Grass Lake in Longyang County

Yuan Dynasty: Tang Gong

Waves of Dongting Lake are aging with the west wind blowing;
Overnight, the hair of goddess Xiangjun is graying.
Drunk, I forgot the sky's reflection in the water is drifting away.
In a boat of beautiful dreams, I am sleeping on the Milky Way.

作者简介

杨慎（1488年—1559年），字用修，号升庵，别号博南山人、洞天真逸、滇南戍史、金马碧鸡老兵等。四川新都（今成都新都区）人；著名文学家，明代三才子之首，东阁大学士杨廷和之子。

杨慎生于书香门第，为人正直，不畏权势；1511年，状元及第（明代四川唯一状元），官翰林院修撰；1524年，谪戍于云南永昌卫。杨慎被放逐滇南三十多年间，关心民间疾苦，不忘国事。1559年，卒于戍所，临终前以"临利不敢先人，见义不敢后身"勉励后人。明熹宗时，追谥"文宪"，世称"杨文宪"。

杨慎博览群书，屹立西南，开启蛮荒，在中国哲学、文化、历史、文学等方面贡献巨大。他是西南地区有史以来著述最为宏富的哲人、作家；后人辑其作为《升庵集》。

杨慎涉猎面广，其诗"浓丽婉至"；其词和散曲清新绮丽；其长篇弹唱叙史之作《二十一史弹词》文笔畅达；其散文古朴高逸。

王夫之称杨慎之诗：三百年来最上乘。陈寅恪曾言：杨用修为人，才高学博，有明一代，罕有其四。

九十一、临江仙·滚滚长江东逝水

明代：杨慎

滚滚长江东逝水，
浪花淘尽英雄。
是非成败转头空。
青山依旧在，
几度夕阳红。

白发渔樵江渚上，
惯看秋月春风。
一壶浊酒喜相逢。
古今多少事，
都付笑谈中。

91. Tune to "Riverside Daffodils"·Rolling, Rolling, the Yangtze River Flows Eastward

Ming Dynasty: Yang Shen

Rolling, rolling, the Yangtze River flows eastward;
Waves outlive heroes always in the world.
All goes empty in a wink, right or wrong, success or failure.
Mountains are as green as ever;
Millions of times, the sunset is red in color.

By the riverside, a fisherman and a woodcutter, both hoary-haired,
Know so well the autumn moon and the spring wind.
They are so happy to meet and are drinking a pot of rice wine.
So many events, either in the past or at present,
Have all become conversation topics of merriment.

作者简介

纳兰性德（1655年—1685年），叶赫那拉氏，字容若，号楞伽山人，满洲正黄旗人，清朝初年词人，与陈维崧、朱彝尊并称"清词三大家"，被誉为"满清第一词人""第一学人"；大学士明珠长子。

纳兰性德文武兼修，1676年，补殿试，赐进士出身。康熙爱其才，授三等侍卫，晋一等侍卫，随康熙出巡；奉旨出使梭龙，考察沙俄侵边情况。纳兰性德淡泊名利，厌恶官场庸俗虚伪。1685年，纳兰性德溘然而逝，年仅三十岁。

纳兰性德词作涉及爱情、边塞、江南等；写景状物以水、荷居多。传世《纳兰词》在其生前即"家家争唱"。纳兰性德词风清新隽秀、哀感顽艳，颇近南唐后主。

王国维赞曰："以自然之眼观物，以自然之舌言情，此初入中原未染汉人风气，故能真切如此，北宋以来，一人而已。"

九十二、蝶恋花·出塞

清代：纳兰性德

今古河山无定据，
画角声中，
牧马频来去。
满目荒凉谁可语？
西风吹老丹枫树。

从来幽怨应无数？
铁马金戈，
青冢黄昏路。
一往情深深几许？
深山夕照深秋雨。

92. Tune to "Butterflies' Love of Flowers"·Out of the Fortress

Qing Dynasty: Nalan Xingde

From time immemorial, a country's rise or destruction is not destined;
In the sound of the military horn painted,
War horses come and go very often.
Who can I talk to amid all the desolation?
The bleak west wind rustles the withering maple trees.

In history, hidden bitterness must be limitless!
Armored horses and golden dagger-axes,
Wang Zhaojun's[1] green-grass-covered grave and the dusk-time road.
How deep is the love in the heart's abode?
The setting sun shines on deep mountains in the late autumn drizzles.

---

[1] **Wang Zhaojun:** a palace lady-in-waiting who lived over 2,000 years ago in the West Han Dynasty in China. She helped secure peace on the turbulent northern border by marrying chieftain of the Hun, a nomadic ethnic group from Central Asia. In 33 B.C., the Hun chieftain paid a respectful visit to Emperor Yuan of the Han Dynasty and asked to marry a Han princess, which was to prove his sincerity to live in peace with the Han people. Emperor Yuan, instead of marrying a princess off to him, offered him five ladies-in-waiting from his harem, and Wang Zhaojun was one of them. After getting married to the Hun chieftain, she convinced him to build a good relationship with the Han people, thus keeping the peace between the Han and the Hun for over half a century. Wang Zhaojun is still commemorated by Chinese people as a peace envoy, who contributed greatly to the friendship between the Han and ethnic groups.

九十三、浣溪沙·谁念西风独自凉

清代：纳兰性德

谁念西风独自凉，
萧萧黄叶闭疏窗，
沉思往事立残阳。

被酒莫惊春睡重，
赌书消得泼茶香，
当时只道是寻常。

93. Tune to "The Yarn-washing Stream"·In the Chilly West Wind, Who Would Care about the Solitary Me?

Qing Dynasty: Nalan Xingde

In the chilly west wind, who would care about the solitary me?
Rustling and falling yellow leaves hide carved windows from view;
Standing in the setting sun, I am lost in missing you.

Drunk, I slept soundly in spring and you are afraid to disturb me;
We, so intimate, had fun betting books[①] and drinking tea;
I thought then it was just so ordinary.

---

① Li Qingzhao (March 13, 1084–May 12, 1155), pseudonym Householder of Yi'an, was a Chinese writer and poet in the Southern Song Dynasty. She had a good memory and liked to read and collect books. Usually, she and her husband Zhao Mingcheng would have tea after dinner. When they were making tea, they would bet books to decide who would be the first one to drink tea. One of them asked the other in which book, in which volume, on which page, and in which line a story was. If the answer was correct, the testee would be the first one to drink tea. They had fun doing that and the winner was very often excited, thus spilling tea occasionally on his/her clothes. In Chinese literary history, the story indicates a good relationship and romance between the couple. The story has become a symbol of romance between couples in China.

九十四、己亥杂诗（其五）

清代：龚自珍

浩荡离愁白日斜，
吟鞭东指即天涯。
落红不是无情物，
化作春泥更护花。

作者简介

龚自珍（1792年—1841年），字璱人，号定庵；仁和（今浙江杭州）人；晚年居昆山羽琌山馆，又号羽琌山民。清代思想家、诗人、文学家和改良主义先驱。

龚自珍生于官宦世家，1829年中进士；曾任内阁中书、礼部主事等职。他主张革除弊政，抵制外国侵略，支持林则徐禁烟。因揭露时弊，触动时忌，遭权贵排挤；1839年春，他辞官南归，次年卒于江苏丹阳云阳书院。

其诗文揭露清朝统治的腐朽，洋溢着爱国热情，被柳亚子誉为"三百年来第一流"。其诗语言自然清丽、瑰丽古奥；思想性和政治性是其诗灵魂，开创了近代诗篇章。

龚自珍是中国传统思想最后一位启蒙思想家，也是中国近代新思想的第一位启蒙思想家。他批判中国政体、教育制度、行为观念等，提出人本主义观点，反对君主专制，关注边疆问题。

龚自珍的思想标志着中国思想启蒙的最高水平和最后阶段。从开始到终结，中国思想的自我启蒙基本维持在同一水平，只是为新王朝的善政提供可借鉴的意见，没有任何新的文明要素。所谓最后阶段，是指在龚自珍之后，再也不能这么思考问题了，中国面临的真实危机必须有新的思想才能解决。

94. Miscellaneous Poems Written in the Year 1839 (5th Poem)

Qing Dynasty: Gong Zizhen

A sea of parting sorrows rolls towards the setting sun;

Pointing my horsewhip eastward, I seem to be in a bleak frontier.

The fallen flowers are not heartless and dry of emotion;

Turning into spring soil, they will nourish more flowers next year.

九十五、己亥杂诗（其九十六）

清代：龚自珍

少年击剑更吹箫，
剑气箫心一例消。
谁分苍凉归棹后，
万千哀乐集今朝。

95. Miscellaneous Poems Written in the Year 1839 (96th Poem)

Qing Dynasty: Gong Zizhen

Young, I mastered sword fighting and played the xiao flute[①];
Together the sword's radiance and my love for flute died out.
Who would have expected that, in life's bleakness, I retired?
Today, like tides, all the sorrow and happiness surged.

[①] **Xiao (flute):** It is generally made of bamboo. It is also sometimes called "dongxiao," "dong" meaning "hole." An ancient name for the xiao is "shuzhudi (lit. vertical bamboo flute)," but the name xiao in ancient times also included the side-blown bamboo flute, dizi.

九十六、己亥杂诗（其一百二十五）

清代：龚自珍

九州生气恃风雷，
万马齐喑究可哀。
我劝天公重抖擞，
不拘一格降人才。

96. Miscellaneous Poems Written in the Year 1839 (125th Poem)

Qing Dynasty: Gong Zizhen

The vitality of China can only be born out of the thunderstorm;
The lifelessness of the whole nation is really a great grief.
I advise the Jade Emperor[①] to keep his spirits up a second time,
And be open-minded on presenting China with talents and relief.

---

① **Jade Emperor:** the supreme deity of Chinese tradition and is known by many names, including Heavenly Grandfather, which originally meant "Heavenly Duke," which is used by commoners; the Jade Lord; the Highest Emperor; Great Emperor of Jade (Yuhuang Shangdi or Yuhuang Dadi); Mr. Heaven (Laotian ye). He governs the cosmos and resides in a magnificent palace in the highest part of heaven along with his large family and entourage of ministers and officials.

九十七、西南联大校歌

近代：罗庸

万里长征，
辞却了五朝宫阙，
暂驻足衡山湘水，
又成离别。
绝徼移栽桢干质，
九州遍洒黎元血。
尽笳吹弦诵在山城，
情弥切。

千秋耻，终当雪。
中兴业，须人杰。
便"一城三户"，
壮怀难折。
多难殷忧新国运，
动心忍性希前哲。
待驱除仇寇复神京，
还燕碣。

作者简介

罗庸（1900年—1950年），字膺中，号习坎，笔名：耘人、佗陵、修梅等，蒙古族；清初扬州八怪之一"两峰山人"罗聘的后人，生于北京；古典文学研究专家和国学家。

1924年，罗庸毕业于北京大学，任职教育部，兼职北大等校；1932年起，任教北大。1937年，抗战爆发，北大、清华、南开合并为长沙临时大学；1938年，西迁昆明，改名国立西南联合大学，罗庸任教授；1939年秋，任北大（已并入西南联大）文科研究所导师，后兼任西南联大中文系主任。1946年秋，三校北返，罗庸任昆明师范学院国文系教授兼系主任。1949年赴重庆，任教于梁漱溟创办的勉仁文学院。1950年病逝于重庆。

罗庸潜心佛学，造诣精深，对西南佛教见解独到。他善于诗词骈文，曾填写《满江红》，作为西南联大校歌。此歌沉痛激荡，慷慨悲壮，与冯友兰所撰《西南联大纪念碑文》堪称双璧。

97. Anthem of National Southwestern Associated University

Modern Times: Luo Yong

Starting a long march of ten thousand miles,
We bade farewell to the capital of five dynasties.
In Hengyang and Changsha, we had a brief stay,
Again, we were on the way.
To remote Yunnan, elite students were moving,
And in China, too many people are bleeding.
Though singing and reciting in the mountain city,
We are more than eager to serve the country faithfully.

The humiliation of a thousand year will be rid of finally,
The prosperity of the country needs talents definitely.
Even though there were only a few hearts left,
We will never, never, never give up till the last fight.
Our motherland suffering, we felt deeply worried.
Willpower strengthened, we struggle as hard as the immortals did.
When the enemies are driven away and the capital is recovered,
We will return to the cities of Beijing and Tianjin.

作者简介

毛泽东（1893年12月26日—1976年9月9日），字润之（原作咏芝，后改润芝），笔名子任。湖南湘潭人。中国革命家、思想家、政治家、战略家、理论家、诗人，中国共产党、中国人民解放军和中华人民共和国的主要缔造者和领袖，毛泽东思想的主要创立者。

从1949年到1976年，毛泽东是中华人民共和国的最高领导人。他对马克思主义的发展、军事理论的贡献以及对共产党的理论贡献被称为毛泽东思想。毛泽东担任过的主要职务几乎全部称为"主席"，所以他被尊称为毛主席。毛泽东被视为现代世界历史中最重要的人物之一，美国《时代》杂志将他评为20世纪最具影响的100人之一。

毛泽东诗词气势磅礴，想象浪漫，文辞华美，沉郁凝重，"偏于豪放，不废婉约（毛泽东）"。与中国历代诗人、词家不同，他是亲历战争的统帅，是在用生命写诗。

毛泽东完成了中国古典诗词的现代转型，他把古典诗词用来反映当代生活和无产阶级革命斗争。毛泽东用诗写史，以史写诗，诗史合一，是为史诗。

毛泽东诗词的艺术境界和气势无人企及。在内容上，毛泽东诗词是现实主义的；在艺术上，他继承了屈原、李白的浪漫主义传统，创造了独有的艺术风格。他善于把想象、比喻、夸张、历史故事、神话传说等融

九十八、沁园春·雪

近代：毛泽东

北国风光，
千里冰封，
万里雪飘。
望长城内外，
惟余莽莽；
大河上下，
顿失滔滔。
山舞银蛇，
原驰蜡象，
欲与天公试比高。
须晴日，
看红装素裹，
分外妖娆。

江山如此多娇，
引无数英雄竞折腰。
惜秦皇汉武，
略输文采；
唐宗宋祖，
稍逊风骚。
一代天骄，
成吉思汗，
只识弯弓射大雕。
俱往矣，
数风流人物，
还看今朝。

98. Tune to "Spring in Qinyuan Garden"·Snow

Modern Times: Mao Zedong

In the north of China, the landscape seen

For thousands of miles, is ice-coated and frozen;

For ten thousand miles around, snow is falling.

Inside and outside the Great Wall I am looking;

On the vast land only snow is working its will.

Upstream and downstream of the Yellow River,

In an instant, has become deadly still.

White ridges are snaking on the mountains as ever;

Mountains, like wax-colored elephants, are running by;

They all want to outgrow the sky.

When a bright and sunny day comes,

The land is putting on reddish and snowy clothes,

And it is exceptionally enchanting like a rose.

Mountains and rivers are so splendid

That countless heroes have been enchanted.

Emperors Qin Shihuang and Han Wu, pitifully,

Were in need of certain literary ability;

Emperors Taizong of Tang and Taizu of Song

Were a bit inferior in literary talent all along.

Nature's chosen man,

Genghis Khan,

Knew only how to shoot vultures with a bow.

They are all bygone legends now.

To number worthy heroes,

Let's have a look at the living ones.

作者简介

（接202页）

为一体，创造出极具特色的艺术形象。毛泽东赞美当代英雄，其评古之诗具有前所未有的大"气"。

美国前国务卿基辛格说："毛泽东的存在本身就是意志的巨大作用的见证。没有任何外在的装饰物可以解释毛泽东所焕发的力量感。我的孩子们谈到流行唱片艺术家身上的一种'颤流'，我得承认自己对此完全感觉不到。但是毛泽东却的确发出力量、权力和意志的颤流。我从来没有遇见过一个人像他具有如此高度集中的不加掩饰的意志力。他身上发出一种几乎可以感觉到的压倒一切的魄力。毛泽东的确能让人体会到力量、权力和意志的共鸣。"

九十九、沁园春·长沙

近代：毛泽东

独立寒秋，
湘江北去，
橘子洲头。
看万山红遍，
层林尽染；
漫江碧透，
百舸争流。
鹰击长空，
鱼翔浅底，
万类霜天竞自由。
怅寥廓，
问苍茫大地，
谁主沉浮？

携来百侣曾游。
忆往昔峥嵘岁月稠。
恰同学少年，
风华正茂；
书生意气，
挥斥方遒。
指点江山，
激扬文字，
粪土当年万户侯。
曾记否，
到中流击水，
浪遏飞舟？

99. Tune to "Spring in Qinyuan Garden"·Changsha

Modern Times: Mao Zedong

I stand alone in autumn chill,

The Xiangjiang River flowing northward at will,

At the head of Orange Island.

I am enjoying the red mountains around;

Forest layers are dyed red.

The whole river is emerald and crystal ahead;

Hundreds of boats are vying with one another.

Eagles are soaring in the sky as ever;

Fish are swimming in the riverbed;

All living things are pursuing freedom with frost overhead.

Before the infinite universe, thoughts surging,

The vast and boundless earth I am asking:

The ups and downs of the world who is deciding?

My companions and I together visited the Island.

In my memory, those days were many and splendid.

We were young schoolmates at that time,

And were in our prime;

Intellectual and high-spirited,

We were energetic and strong-minded.

Commenting on the problems of the country,

We wrote to praise or attack passionately,

And regarded the warlords as dung and dirt.

Do you all still remember that

We swam in the middle of the river,

And waves were preventing the boats from sailing further.

一百、卜算子·咏梅

近代：毛泽东

风雨送春归，
飞雪迎春到。
已是悬崖百丈冰，
犹有花枝俏。

俏也不争春，
只把春来报。
待到山花烂漫时，
她在丛中笑。

欣赏笔记

100. Tune to "Song of the Fortune-Teller"·Ode to Plum Blossoms

Modern Times: Mao Zedong

The wind and the rain have sent spring away;
The falling snow is ushering in spring.
On the surface of the high cliffs, icicles have formed;
Beautiful branches of plum blossoms are yet blooming.

Though beautiful, they mean not to compete in beauty pageants;
They just want to be harbingers of spring.
When mountain flowers are beautifully blooming,
Among them, plum blossoms are sweetly smiling.

参考书目

1. 古诗文网 https://so.gushiwen.org/
2. 360 百科 https://baike.so.com/
3. 诗词名句网 http://www.shicimingju.com/
4. 知乎 https://www.zhihu.com/
5. 《庄子全译》（张耿光译注），贵州出版社，1991 年 7 月第 1 版

后记

对热爱诗歌的人来说，与诗相伴，是人生最美的遇见。诗歌是中国传统教育的一部分，所以，在中国人的精神生活中，诗歌占有非常重要的地位。就诗歌来说，言志、抒情和记事是其主要功能。

经典诗歌是中华优秀传统文化的一部分，对建设当代中国道德秩序和价值体系具有重要意义。在当今世界，国家间文化交流、交融、交锋日益频繁，传承和弘扬中华文化的优秀传统，是保持文化独立性的重要途径。

《中国经典诗词选英译》旨在为国内外英语学习者和读者，以及翻译学习者提供中国经典诗词英译的另一种选择，帮助他/她们提高鉴赏能力，开阔阅读视野，感受中华诗歌文化的魅力。译者深爱中国古典诗词，学习英语多载，教学之余，感于中国古典诗歌之美，试以英文译之。今结而成集，即将面世，恐贻笑大方，故诚惶诚恐。翻译过程中，鲜参考他人之译文，若有错译，全因译者功力不逮所致，还望读者见谅。

二十五年前，求学之季，译者曾通读许渊冲先生译著《不朽之诗》，特在此向先生致敬。

在译诗、编辑直至出版过程中，我得到了许多人的帮助和支持。在此，我要表示真诚的谢意：

非常感谢云南师范大学外国语学院冯智文教授、彭庆华教授、李丽生教授、李昌银教授、杨燕教授、王庆玲教授、邹霞教授、袁刚教授、薛文俊、周辉和刘婵老师等的支持和帮助，以及云南师范大学外国语学院对译诗出版给予的资金支持。

非常感谢中国人民大学出版社给予我机会出版本书。

特别感谢美国专家包琼女士通读译稿，对译诗提出了宝贵意见和修改、完善的办法，确保了译诗的质量。

特别感谢李正栓教授！在此，真诚感谢河北师范大学外国语学院著名学者李正栓教授的鼓励和支持。他在百忙之中，抽出宝贵的时间为本书作序，对此我深表感激。他的学术和翻译成就一直为学人所敬佩，是我学习的楷模。

最后，感谢我的妻子和女儿一直以来的爱和支持，是她们的鼓励和理解才使此书得以完稿。感谢我的父母使我能够得到最好的教育，还有我的弟弟妹妹，以及其他亲人长久以来的支持。

尹绍东

2019年6月26日于昆明文华苑

AFTERWORD

For poetry lovers, it is the most beautiful encounter in life to live with poetry. Poetry is part of Chinese traditional education. In Chinese people's spiritual life, poetry plays a very important role. Seen from poetry's themes, poetry is mainly about poets' aspirations, love and emotions, or daily life.

Classic Chinese poetry is part of the Chinese excellent traditional culture and it is of great significance to the construction of the contemporary Chinese moral order and value system. Now, in the world, cultural communication, blending, and conflict have become increasingly common. Therefore, the inheritance and promotion of Chinese excellent traditional culture is a critical measure to maintain cultural distinction and independence.

A Collection of Classic Chinese Poems and Lyrics is compiled and translated to be another choice for English learners, readers, and students who are learning translation in or outside China to have some knowledge of classic Chinese poetry. This will help them improve their abilities to appreciate poetry, broaden their horizons, and discover the charm of Chinese poetry culture. I deeply love classical Chinese poetry and have learned English for many years. As an English teacher, in my spare time, I tried to translate some classical Chinese poems into English due to my love of their beauty. Now, I have collected my translations for publication. Apprehensive that I might be laughed at, criticized or even attacked by great scholars or well-known translators, I have been very cautious in my work. In the translating process, I rarely went to other translations for reference, so if there are any errors, mistakes or misunderstandings, it is just because of the fact that I am still not qualified enough for such a task. It is my hope that I should be forgiven by the readers.

Twenty five years ago, as a college student, I read Professor Xu Yuanchong's English translation book: *Song of the Immortals*. I herein have the greatest respect for

AFTERWORD

Professor Xu.

In the process of translating, editing and publishing those poems, I have been helped and supported by many colleagues, friends, and family members. I wish now to express my sincere gratitude to all of them:

I would like to acknowledge the professors and associate professors in the School of Foreign Languages and Literature of Yunnan Normal University for their continued support and encouragement. They are Feng Zhiwen, Peng Qinghua, Li Lisheng, Li Changyin, Yang Yan, Wang Qingling, Zou Xia, Yuan Gang, Xue Wenjun, Zhou Hui, and Liu Chan. My thanks also go to the School of Foreign Languages and Literature of Yunnan Normal University for its financial support for the publication of the present book.

My gratitude is also due to China Renmin University Press for granting me the opportunity to publish the book.

Special thanks go to American expert Ms. Joan Cecile Boulerice for her reading through the draft and offering her advice on revision, thus perfecting the translation and ensuring the quality of the book.

Special thanks go to Professor Li Zhengshuan! I herein extend my sincere appreciation to him, a great scholar of the School of Foreign Studies of Hebei Normal University, for his encouragement and support. I am indebted to him for his generosity in sparing his valuable time to write the preface of the book. He has been admired for his academic and translation achievements and I have been trying hard to emulate him.

Finally, I would like to thank my wife and daughter for their love and continued support. It is their encouragement and understanding that make possible the completion of the book. In addition, I would like to thank my parents for ensuring that I received the best education possible, as well as my brother, sister and other relatives for their continued support.

Yin Shaodong
June 26, 2019, Wenhua Yuan, Kunming

中国人民大学出版社外语出版分社读者信息反馈表

尊敬的读者：

　　感谢您购买和使用中国人民大学出版社外语出版分社的 ＿＿＿＿＿＿＿＿ 一书，我们希望通过这张小小的反馈卡来获得您更多的建议和意见，以改进我们的工作，加强我们双方的沟通和联系。我们期待着能为更多的读者提供更多的好书。

　　请您填妥下表后，寄回或传真回复我们，对您的支持我们不胜感激！

1. 您是从何种途径得知本书的：
　　□书店　　　□网上　　　□报纸杂志　　　□朋友推荐
2. 您为什么决定购买本书：
　　□工作需要　　□学习参考　　□对本书主题感兴趣　　□随便翻翻
3. 您对本书内容的评价是：
　　□很好　　　□好　　　□一般　　　□差　　　□很差
4. 您在阅读本书的过程中有没有发现明显的专业及编校错误，如果有，它们是：
　　＿＿＿＿＿＿＿＿＿＿＿＿＿＿＿＿＿＿＿＿＿＿＿＿＿＿＿＿＿＿＿＿＿＿＿＿＿
　　＿＿＿＿＿＿＿＿＿＿＿＿＿＿＿＿＿＿＿＿＿＿＿＿＿＿＿＿＿＿＿＿＿＿＿＿＿
　　＿＿＿＿＿＿＿＿＿＿＿＿＿＿＿＿＿＿＿＿＿＿＿＿＿＿＿＿＿＿＿＿＿＿＿＿＿
5. 您对哪些专业的图书信息比较感兴趣：
　　＿＿＿＿＿＿＿＿＿＿＿＿＿＿＿＿＿＿＿＿＿＿＿＿＿＿＿＿＿＿＿＿＿＿＿＿＿
　　＿＿＿＿＿＿＿＿＿＿＿＿＿＿＿＿＿＿＿＿＿＿＿＿＿＿＿＿＿＿＿＿＿＿＿＿＿
　　＿＿＿＿＿＿＿＿＿＿＿＿＿＿＿＿＿＿＿＿＿＿＿＿＿＿＿＿＿＿＿＿＿＿＿＿＿
6. 如果方便，请提供您的个人信息，以便于我们和您联系（您的个人资料我们将严格保密）：
　　您供职的单位：＿＿＿＿＿＿＿＿＿＿＿＿＿＿＿＿＿＿＿＿＿＿＿＿＿＿＿＿＿
　　您教授的课程（教师填写）：＿＿＿＿＿＿＿＿＿＿＿＿＿＿＿＿＿＿＿＿＿＿＿
　　您的通信地址：＿＿＿＿＿＿＿＿＿＿＿＿＿＿＿＿＿＿＿＿＿＿＿＿＿＿＿＿＿
　　您的电子邮箱：＿＿＿＿＿＿＿＿＿＿＿＿＿＿＿＿＿＿＿＿＿＿＿＿＿＿＿＿＿

　　请联系我们：贾乐凯　　吴振良　　黄婷　　程子殊　　王琼　　鞠方安
　　电话：010-62515580，62515538，62512737，62513265，62515573，62515576
　　传真：010-62514961
　　E-mail：jialk@crup.com.cn　　　wuzl@crup.com.cn　　　huangt@crup.com.cn
　　　　　　chengzsh@crup.com.cn　　crup_wy@163.com　　　jufa@crup.com.cn
　　通信地址：北京市海淀区中关村大街甲59号文化大厦15层　　邮编：100872
　　中国人民大学出版社外语出版分社